Destiny Detours

A Testimony of Faith through the Fire

September Rein

WESTBOW
PRESS®
A DIVISION OF THOMAS NELSON
& ZONDERVAN

WestBow Press books may be ordered through booksellers or by contacting:

WestBow Press
A Division of Thomas Nelson & Zondervan
1663 Liberty Drive
Bloomington, IN 47403
www.westbowpress.com
1 (866) 928-1240

ISBN: 978-1-9736-7550-1 (sc)
ISBN: 978-1-9736-7551-8 (hc)
ISBN: 978-1-9736-7549-5 (e)

Library of Congress Control Number: 2019914573

Print information available on the last page.

WestBow Press rev. date: 10/22/2019

In this beauty-for-ashes story, I share from my heart the revelations I received and strength I gained from God as He took my hand and heart on a journey walking through fire but coming out the other side without even the smell of smoke.

My prayer is that anyone searching for hope in their trials or a light at the end of their tunnels will be encouraged as I share how God refined me like pure gold is refined and that as you read through these pages of my reality and God's truth, you'll find God move in your very own situation.

I pray that you find yourself stepping into God's plan for you regardless of the impossibilities and that you see yourself flourish like a flower in the desert and you seek God.

I pray that God will give you personal revelation as you seek His Word for yourself and whatever circumstance you find yourself in, whether you put yourself in it or were forced into it from the ripple effects of someone else's choices.

I pray that you grow deeper in His love for you, His real love. And, God, I pray that as these words are read whatever it is that has found you here to be reading these pages, you see God for who He really is, not a judgmental, harsh-spoken, cranky man but a kind, gracious, good, loving Father.

Your pain today is for your purpose tomorrow.

I dedicate this book to my two children and all the women who don't have voices of their own yet. And I thank my village from the depths of my soul, those whom God brought alongside me to lift my arms when I couldn't carry myself and who have helped raise my children in the ways they should go, facing toward Jesus and knowing how much they're loved and believed in.

About Me

I was always the problem child, or so I thought. Growing up as the youngest of three sisters, I was apparently always annoying them and their friends in some way or another, although that's what younger sibling do, right?

Whether I was throwing witchetty grubs at them to get a reaction or getting my hands into their moisturizer creams and using their perfumes as I got older, being the youngest, I always found a way to get myself in trouble and dobbed on.

Throughout primary school, I was a very busy child and not so easily able to concentrate for long periods in class because all I wanted was lunchtime to hurry up so I could play. What I can remember most is that I was the sporty girl who was good at everything that was sports, and when I say everything, I mean everything.

I once made the district basketball team, and that tryout was my first *ever* time playing basketball. Maybe I was destined to be some sort of athlete, you'd say, or maybe I just had the spirit to not give in or give up, and mix that determination with my ability to learn on the go was the perfect combination for an athlete maybe or maybe just a girl with a strong will to keep going even when there seemed to be no path to follow..

I wouldn't say I was an overachieving, attention-loving, basking-in-the-glory kind of kid. If anything, I hated (and still do today) the spotlight and attention.

We'd have the school assembly, and I'd get the first-place blue ribbon for literally every sports award for my age group. From running to swimming, high jump to long jump, if you name it, I was first at it.

All I really remember in primary school was sports.

I suppose you can say I found what I was good at, and the passion for sports did something in my little spirit that stood out and rose up to say, *You can do this; you're unstoppable.*

And I totally believed it. I knew that if I set my mind to it, I'd conquer it, and if I failed, it didn't seem to faze me.

Oh, how I wish I still naturally had that same young spirit without doubt distracting my adult years.

I distinctly remember an athletics day when I'd have been about ten or eleven years old, and of course, I was in every race that was on offer and coming first in all the heats.

It came to the first final, and it was the four-hundred-meter race where you run around the oval track, I remember that I was in the outside lane, the one closest to the crowd of peers and parents on the sidelines.

Bang! Off went the start gun, and the smell of gunpowder filled my senses, and off I went with my little legs running at a fast but paced balance so I could save my energy boost for after the bend to the last leg. I had done this every year since I was old enough to be in the school athletics carnivals and, even more so, done every race, so it was safe to say I was in my prime of running for a primary-aged kid.

My feet pounded the grass track beneath my joggers. As I approached the bend and started to hear the crowd cheering, I felt the sprint kick in. Off I went, my legs running so fast, my head thrown back. And to make up for the speed and my head, I leaned forward, but before I knew it, I'd completely thrown myself off balance and tumbled in what felt like slow motion, flat on my face.

To be completely honest, I saw it coming in the moment, but I was running so fast I couldn't stop it from happening. It was literally like a movie scene with the clumsy slow-motion fall when the entire crowd gasps and holds their breath for me. It felt like minutes of just lying sprawled on the grass trying to figure out what just happened and what to do next, but it was only a few seconds, and by the time

I looked up, the last runner has passed me, but I jumped up and finished the race.

No tears, no tantrums, no feelings of despair, I just got up and did what I instinctively thought to do which was finish the race. I think at that single moment of what I now would call a failure, in my childhood life I unknowingly made a choice and commitment to that race and the rest of my life decisions that if I failed or fell to just get up and finish the race. I had no idea of how much I'd need to be reminded of that in my adult years.

This natural inclination or maybe default setting has stuck with me throughout my days from the smallest to the tallest trials I've faced so far in life, my worst day yet has not killed me, and because it hasn't killed me, it has done two things. It has made me stronger, and it has taught me either what to do or what not to do.

chapter 1

When I Fall, I Can Fall
to the Arms of Jesus

Have you ever heard some news that blows the wind right out of you and stops you dead in your tracks? Maybe news a loved one has passed on. Maybe a phone call from the school office that starts off with, "Your child is on the way to the hospital." Possibly it's the dreaded call from your boss that you were hoping not to receive. Or maybe it includes lies and deceit coming from the one who should care about you the most.

Or maybe it's not even a call but a face-to-face conversation with the only person you want to trust apart from your spouse. That person is about to break the trust you're trying to build and turn your whole world not just upside down but inside out.

When I started writing this book, I prayed that it would help anyone searching madly—as I was—for hope from someone who had been through something similar before. The only thing was I couldn't find anyone who had been through exactly what I was going through. Here I was, a young, naive wife, a mother, and a daughter who had been in ministry for ten years. I had been on staff at the local church, had a team I was leading, and had families I was pastoring. I also had a circle of friends and relatives who thought I had it all together.

I felt so much pressure from the world to have it all perfectly together, and I was so ashamed of what happened behind closed doors that I couldn't even imagine what it would be like to tell someone—or how to even find someone to tell. The Enemy's voice of shame in the back of my head told me all these people looking up to me would say that it was my fault, that there was something wrong with me, that I must have done something to push away my husband and make him mad. The list of lies goes on and on, and I believed them for over a decade.

I've been careful not to share anything that I think could be taken the wrong way, that makes me look like I'm a victim or that blames my estranged husband because that's not my goal. The only reason I said yes to writing this book was to share something that may connect my experience with someone else's and give *hope* that when readers come out the other side of this, God will restore them to the fullness of His perfect plan on their lives. And they *will* be stronger, braver, wiser, and refined and pure like gold after coming through the fire.

I'd heard the stories and come across verses about God refining His people through the fires and trials. These verses are about silver and gold and coming through fire not smelling of smoke. They're always so encouraging but not so personal. And never before had I been through a fire so fierce that I actually thought there was no way out, apart from coming out in chunks of ember. I couldn't see how I'd survive emotionally or mentally. But if I did, I'd for sure not just be scarred for the rest of my life but with open, gushing wounds.

I need to tell you before you read anymore that not only did I survive, but also I'm thriving. God doesn't bring you to the foot of the furnace just to leave you there alone. God is always with you. When you feel most alone, get in His Word. That's what will sustain you. Nothing else will. Not your best friend, not your pastor, not the box of chocolates or bottle of wine, and not even that reality TV show you binge-watch to feel better about your own life. Let me get real for a moment. I tried them all, and the only one that works is knowing the Word of God deep in my heart and soul.

God doesn't cause the trials and troubles we go through in life, but He can turn around any trouble we face for His good plan and purpose over our lives—if we're willing to let Him and to follow His way out, not trying to make it on our own. God can use the fire to melt away all the dirt and unwanted, impure parts of our lives just the way goldsmiths make twenty-four-karat gold. They refine it by melting it in a furnace of fire so all the impure parts come away, and what's left is pure gold.

Get your highlighter out and search God's Word for your own personal revelation on how He'll lift you up and restore you.

There's only so much you can learn from another person, read in a book, or get from a podcast. There comes a time when you need to hear God's wisdom for yourself about your circumstances. He'll always be right there waiting to speak to you. Just take the time to listen.

Confess the word of God, and speak Gods truth and promises out. Reading the Word out loud is a choice of weapon you may not see the effects of, but it's powerful.

> See, I have refined you, though not as silver; I have tested you in the furnace of affliction. Isaiah 48:10

> For you, God, tested us; you refined us like silver. Psalm 66:10

> Is not my word like fire, declares the Lord, and like a hammer that breaks a rock in pieces? Jeremiah 23:29

> The crucible for silver and the furnace for gold, but the Lord tests the heart. Proverbs 17:3

Remove the dross from the silver, and a silversmith can produce a vessel. Proverbs 25:4

And the words of the Lord are flawless, like silver purified in a crucible, like gold refined seven times. Psalm 12:6

But he knows the way that I take; when he has tested me, I will come forth as gold. Job 23:10

See, I have refined you, though not as silver; I have tested you in the furnace of affliction. Isaiah 48:10

He will sit as a refiner and purifier of silver; he will purify the Levites and refine them like gold and silver. Then the Lord will have men who will bring offerings in righteousness. Malachi 3:3

When you pass through the waters, I will be with you; and when you pass through the rivers, they will not sweep over you. When you walk through the fire, you will not be burned; the flames will not set you ablaze. Isaiah 43:2

The word *refine* is a verb meaning "to remove impurities or unwanted elements from a substance, typically as part of an industrial process."

When researching how gold is refined, I learned there's more than one way. But the oldest way I found is through fire. The process gold has to go through to be refined into twenty-four-karat gold is a lesson in itself. I've learned it's similar to the fire God walked me through. It had me in pieces the same way all the elements are separated when refining gold in fire. All the impurities separate, and what comes out through the burning fire is pure gold.

I was so broken, my mind was so clouded, and my eyes were so glazed over with a thick film of shame and fear that I couldn't even see it happening.

If you're reading this book, you might know God enough to know He loves us so much that He would never make us do anything. The fact He loves us so much is why we have the freedom and free will to make our own choices. God knows every possible outcome to every choice we could ever make. He can change the world in less than a split second to still turn people's bad or evil choices into good for the ones who love and honor Him.

As I look back to what i thought was the worst year of my life and would not be able to get out alive from, i remember the reoccuring moments of relief as i would get into the shower and realizing I finally had a moment to myself, and it would get real. I'd feel the hurt that turned into an agonizing pain that often ended with me on my knees crying to God. It would just come out in groans as I asked why, how, and when the pain would stop.

Before my world as I knew it fell apart, I felt so alone. I had a husband who'd just disappear. He'd go on work trips with no notice, and in what felt like overnight, he stopped talking to me about anything. When I asked about any details of anything personal, I was faced with a brick wall reply of "Nothing" or "Stop being so psycho and stupid."

It was like a roundabout leading to a dead end of shame, but I had no idea I was in it. I'd gone through thirteen years of emotional abuse that I was in denial about. I just blamed his past to justify his actions and words.

I no longer trusted the one person I'd trusted the most, so how was I supposed to trust anyone? *How can I tell anyone what is going on in my life?* I wondered daily in what seemed like a prison in my own head. I constantly told myself there was no point because I didn't even know what was going on, so how could I even talk to someone else about it?

Let's be honest here for a minute: I found that I was at the breaking point in my sanity.

Not only did I think I was going crazy because of what was constantly blasted at me. The things I saw or heard in reality, like a text message or an email, were deleted, and then I heard a simple "No, it wasn't there," or "It didn't happen," were the only answers I ever got, no more and no less.

I was stuck at a point where everyone else around me, friends and family, were putting together the pieces that I didn't want to see, let alone put together. I was married to a man who was living a double life.

You see, I was so full of shame and so scared to be a single parent because of what others would think of me. Divorce was so foreign, and unknown to me, then on top I wondered what was wrong with me that I was willing to settle for an unhealthy marriage and family, with myself and my children being poisoned from the inside out and not living life anywhere near where God had planned.

I tried so desperately to control the situation by changing anything possible I thought was wrong with me.

All the thoughts were lined up and ready to go. I didn't even need to search for them. They even had their own small voice that sounded very familiar telling me:

There must be something wrong with the way I look.

But I don't know what to change.

I'm not doing good enough to please him as a wife should please her husband.

That has to be it!

I'm too controlling over him!

Hmmm, that's strange, though, because deep down inside, I feel like it's the opposite, but I must just expect too much of him. Maybe even when he says he wants me to plan all the outings and kids' days, he must really want do it.

I'm not nice enough. I'm always angry and mean!

But hang on. That's weird because all my family and friends say the opposite. Oh, well, better make sure I don't question him anymore or challenge the morals and values we had.

I'm too loud and just plain annoying!

Stop being so ridiculous when I find things funny, and tone it down, girl. I can do that easy! Don't feel sad about it. I'll just tone it down near him and only laugh with my friends because they don't seem to mind. In fact, they kind of say the opposite of what he says. Oh well, It's my fault. I need to fix that part of me too.

Stop teaching the kids to be "psycho" with your dancing and singing, especially at night before bed!

Ok, I need to tone it way down with the dancing and singing at home and definitely don't do it in public or in the car. He just hates that. Plus, it makes him angry.

I share this because now I can see just how ridiculous that all really was.

Not even just what he said to me but that I actually tried to change, cover up, and hide the treasure God put inside me.

Don't get me wrong. Sometimes we do need to tone it down in certain situations. Meaning don't live your life as an over-the-top, peaking-on-air drama queen.

God made us all unique and perfect. You won't fit in my mold, and I won't fit in yours, so don't even try.

I see it like this: even though I use the word *mold*, there actually is no mold. But if we let God shape us, He'll mold and shape you perfectly. From the moment, we're born until the moment we come home to Him into eternity, we're forever changing, growing, and morphing into a different shape because that's just how He created us.

He puts in a few ingredients of gifts and talents specifically for you, and then the rest is up to us to continue to grow, learn, and morph into what God has called us to become as His hand gently guides and shape us. Not one of us is the same or will be the same, and that's the beauty of it.

At the time, I couldn't see the terrible choices I was making to change or hide all the treasures that God had tucked away inside of me, and the worst part of it all was that all this was to try and please a person. The quicker in life we can learn to not be people pleasers and to know that God has approved and qualified you for all He has purposed you for, the freer we will be.

The more I looked at what I wanted to try to change, the more I focused on pleasing the people around me, which ultimately meant the more my eyes were taken away from Jesus.

And that right there was a problem.

When you fix your eyes on Jesus, everything around you fades, and the pinpoint of your focus is God.

I found the more I was distracted by the things around me, the more my focus and thoughts slowly drifted off Jesus and onto the problems of my every day, without me even noticing. If I wasn't careful to catch where my thoughts and focus were going, my problems were being magnified bigger than God.

This is an ongoing daily choice that I need to still choose to focus on Jesus and not all the hiccups and speed bumps of everyday life because that's exactly what speed bumps in the form of small daily problems do—they slow you down.

Now I'm more aware of it, so I can snap myself back into focus on what actually matters most and link it to keeping my eyes fixed on Jesus and all that He has for me in that day.

> I tell you, my friends, do not be afraid of those who kill the body and after that can do no more. But I will show you whom you should fear: Fear him who, after your body has been killed, has authority to throw you into hell. Yes, I tell you, fear him.

> Are not five sparrows sold for two pennies? Yet not one of them is forgotten by God. Indeed, the very hairs of your head are all numbered. Don't be

afraid; you are worth more than many sparrows.
Luke 12:4–7

Let me be the first to tell you if no one has ever told you before: you can trust God wholeheartedly. He doesn't give you just a small portion of His love. He loves you wholeheartedly and unconditionally.

There's actually no one who can or will ever love you more than God does. There's nothing in your past that will make his love for you any less. You don't need to prove anything to Him. He loves you just the way you are right now, and you can trust Him. You can trust God having no fear of punishment.

"What if I fall?" you ask. If you fall, don't let it take your breath away. Close your eyes raise your head and fall into God's arms. And remember this: you might just fly instead of fall.

chapter 2

God Loves You from the Beginning to the End

High school was a whole new ball game for me. The first thing that put me way out of my comfort zone was the fact that I was enrolled in an all-girls school. In the years to come, I'm sure it shaped me for the better, as there were no boys to be distracted by, to worry about what I looked like, or to be concerned about the way I acted. And since I didn't have any brothers, you'd assume I'd fit right in, right?

Wrong. I felt so unsure how to make friends with girls. My social skills from the primary school years included playing sports with the boys, and although I had two older sisters, I was labelled the tomboy even at home.

During primary school, I spent all my time and energy playing sports. My lunchtimes were spent being the only girl standing in the corner of a yellow-painted square on the asphalt to play handball or running full speed to the grass field to make sure I'd have a place on the lunch soccer team with all the boys.

In saying that, I remember myself being one of the best. Now maybe that's only according to my memory, but the memories seem to be pretty clear. If you were a handball player from my era, you might remember the serious games were played with a ball where the furry outer layer was removed from the tennis ball and only the bare, dark-brown skin was left, which would sting your palm as you slammed the ball over the line and smashed your opponent! I promise I'm actually not *that* competitive.

In looking back at all this, it makes sense to me now that I wasn't sure how to make friends with girls because that's just it—you need to have actually made friends with girls. Boys were not as much drama for me, well, not in my primary school days anyway. You just kind of hung out and played. It was laid back, chilled out, and you all just fit in, although boys like to stir up and get reactions, which is what I was also good at doing to my sisters at home. The boys didn't gossip or viciously tease, which in my personal experience the young girls did.

I still have memories of name-calling and whispers that were passed around about me from the girls' groups because I was a "tomboy," my last name was the same as an animal, and even because my skin tone was darker.

Maybe they were intimidated by me because I was better at their favorite sport, or maybe they were jealous because I was hanging out and effortlessly playing handball, soccer, or whatever the lunchtime game was with the boy they were crushing on. Who knows? But what I did know is that an easy way to deal with that for me was to just avoid friendships with girls.

So I didn't have a best friend growing up, but is it important for a child to have one specific best friend above other friendships? I don't know, but what I do know as an adult now is that it most definitely helped shape that bad-girl, no-one-messes-with-me front I could put on in one second if needed.

Anyway, going back to making friends in high school, I can't actually pinpoint a memory of who my first friend was or how it came about. But the struggle was real for me making friends. I remember the first few weeks when school started. I floated around the playground just watching the different groups that were clicking and connecting or accepting and rejecting each other (however you want to call it.)

Up until the year I dropped out of high school, I was still a group floater. I think it worked best for me and my outer shell of being little miss bad girl, too cool for school.

That first year of high school really shaped a part of me. I suppose I wouldn't be the person I am today otherwise, but when looking back, I can see the influence on my life that I still doubted until recent years.

My parents were always concerned about who I hung out with and who I was being influenced by, but little did they know at the time, I was the influencer of others. I'm not at all proud to admit this, but it's all part of who I was in the past that God radically changed me from when I met Jesus in my later years.

I was that kid who hustled cigarettes and other things on the playground from friends who had parents who smoked, and I somehow ended up as the one to be scared of if you had a fight with another girl at school. My name was used as the friend who would "protect" you if you were in a fight. Was this using leadership well? I'd say most definitely not, but I had no idea the influence and plan and purpose for my life back then.

I distinctly remember conversations with peers, and thoughts of my own were often about how we couldn't wait to grow up. Grow up and do what? Who knows? But it was just to grow up.

My life was self-centered, like most kids and young adult lives are, yet I yearned for purpose and to know my calling in life. I always had this deeply buried feeling that I was created to not just change the world but be part of something so much bigger than I could ever fathom. I knew my calling was to be part of something far bigger than myself, far bigger and wilder than I could ever imagine in my wildest dreams. I just had no idea what that meant, how to get to it, or even why I felt it deep inside. It was just in there, burning like a flame since as young as I can remember—even as a four-year-old lying on my back on the trampoline, gazing through the clouds up into the sky, wondering about a God I didn't yet know but distinctively feeling His very presence.

I was never the teachers' favorite student, and I remember purposefully acting up in scripture (religion) class. In my mind, it was good that I floated between the social circles because it meant I always had one of the brighter/smarter kids I strategically sat myself with to copy the homework that I hadn't done. I don't ever recall doing any type of homework at home throughout my entire high schooling, which was definitely one reason why I didn't feel qualified to be writing this very book. But I've learned we don't qualify ourselves because God already has.

> It is not that we think we are qualified to do anything on our own. Our qualification comes from God. 2 Corinthians 3:5

I have no idea how I got away with no homework at home because I was brought up with two older sisters who were both high achieving and even selective school material. They were the type of sisters who, every time I ended up in the school office, I could hear the sighs of other teachers. "Oh, that's the younger sister." I don't remember ever really being acknowledged by my own name at school when it came to being judged against my older sisters.

Although I thought it never really bothered me, I just realized I wasn't the same as them academically and never thought it was a good idea to strive to do something that I thought wasn't in me. I think it created a mind-set for me that I just wasn't the sharpest tool in the shed, and that was OK by my standards because I had other things going for me, like my bad-girl personality. Who knows where that was going to get me? But I clung to that sucker like it was my identity to live by.

By the end of year ten at school, I was a dropout, and I decided I wasn't going to continue with my school education as I wasn't getting much education out of it anyway (I do not condone that attitude). That said, it was my own fault, not the school's.

My future plan wasn't clear, although I hadn't made a decision about what I wanted to do for the rest of my life. All I knew was that I wasn't a textbook learner and I couldn't sit in class for one more day. I longed to get my hands into something, and I yearned to make a difference somewhere and somehow, so that was my mission at sixteen years of age—to just get out there in the big, wide world and get on with it. I'm so grateful I had parents who believed in and supported me as long as I found a job that I took seriously, although they completely disagreed with me dropping out of school. So off I went, sixteen years old searching for what I wanted to do with my life.

Now as I look back, I'd say that time was a fork in the road toward my destiny, where I had the choice to follow on from the destructive teenage years I'd been living in high school, full of nothing productive, just cigarettes, joints, the next party, and binge drinking.

By this stage in my life, I'd met the boy of my dreams, the one, the only. I was sixteen, and he was seventeen when we met, and we knew we were getting married. Nothing was stopping us. If we both had been over the legal age, I'm sure we'd have disappeared to somewhere, the equivalent of a Vegas wedding. With what money? Who knows? All we knew was we "loved" each other, whatever we thought "love" was, and that was all we needed, right?

Yes, of course, you need love, but I'd also say to any other sixteen-year-old girl that you need to grow and dig deep into God's love for yourself and get some life experience before you even think you're deeply, madly in love with a boy/man. And don't even get me started on life experience, sweet one.

So, bottom line, don't run away with your boyfriend. It doesn't really matter how old you are, but if you're running away with a man, you need to stop, and you need to ask yourself what exactly you fear that you're running away from.

There is no fear in love. But perfect love drives out
fear, because fear has to do with punishment. The
one who fears is not made perfect in love. 1 John 4:18

The perfect love we'll search for with all our beings—and
sometimes all our lives—is God's love. I remember being a brand-
new Christian and totally understanding for the first time what that
hole in my life and heart was meant to be filled with.

Previously when I heard other Christians talking about using a
person to fill the holes in their lives, I always thought it was some
strange saying or something just plain weird. I was so blinded, even
though I myself was living my own life stuffing as many material
things as I could find down my own hole, which was more of a
bottomless pit to fill.

I shoved everything down there as fast as I could, starting with
a boy who gave me attention and on to buying clothes and shoes,
pouring some drinking and drugs down there, along with comfort
eating, and let's top that off with attracting other unhealthy people.

I got so good at filling my bottomless pit at the right time. I look
back now and realize that I looked pretty happy and satisfied on the
outside, so I'm not surprised at all that certain other unstable people
followed on from my lead.

There's a problem when you have two, three, or even more
people feeding off each other in their unhealthy ways and habits. It
becomes a downward spiral, a roundabout of death and destruction.
It almost works the same way as when we are being Christ-like and
helping build each other up and spurring each other on, speaking
life and moving forward.

As iron sharpens iron, so one person sharpens
another. Proverbs 27:17

Some types of relationships and behaviors pull us down, and
whether you want to or not, you'll learn bad habits and behaviors

from each other the same way you do when you surround yourself with people who have healthy habits.

> Don't hang out with angry people; don't keep company with hotheads. Bad temper is contagious—don't get infected. Proverbs 22:24–25

> Do not be deceived: Bad company ruins good morals. 1 Corinthians 15:33

> Whoever walks with the wise becomes wise, but the companion of fools will suffer harm. Proverbs 13:20

> Escape quickly from the company of fools; they're a waste of your time, a waste of your words. Proverbs 14:7

> My son, if sinful men entice you, do not give in to them. Proverbs 1:10

> One who is righteous is a guide to his neighbor, but the way of the wicked leads them astray. Proverbs 12:26

When I was blinded in sin, I wouldn't have been able to see any of the truth in these verses, even if the greatest Bible scholar in the world had broken them down for me.

But now, my sweet friend, now I see, and I have no excuse to not be aware of the hole that only God fills in my life with His perfect love. And might I add that He fits perfectly into the hole. There's no gap or space if His love is there. Nothing else needs to or can slip between because there are no gaps in my bottomless pit of shoe shopping and binge eating late at night once the kids go to bed.

None of that would ever give me the feeling I longed for that wasn't just a temporary good feeling.

I remember that overwhelming sense, the feeling of joy and wholeness, the day I accepted Jesus into my heart. I couldn't explain what was happening. I had no clue what was going on.

It was the same preacher who had been bringing the word every week in the morning service that I had been attending, but to be honest, I can't even remember what the message was about. All I knew was my heart was beating faster and slower at the same time throughout the entire message, and the moment he made the altar call, I shot my hand up in the air, and my eyes started leaking like a faucet had been turned on full force and the handle had broken off.

In that moment, it was like my hand shooting up had broken something that was hanging over my life. It was like my hand broke the seal of the bubble I was in, and I felt a freedom I'd never felt or experienced before. It was so real, thick, and tangible.

The few years before this life-defining moment happened at the age of eighteen, I seemed to spiral down faster than ever before, and I saw no possible way out or upward.

chapter 3

God's Love Is Waiting Patiently Yet Fiercely for You to Respond

From the ages of sixteen to eighteen, I had no drive in life apart from the next social event, weekend party, or backyard BBQ, and if there was nothing of the sort planned, I wondered what time we'd meet at the club for drinks after work. Now when I look back, I sigh and wonder how I thought that was a life full of purpose. I find it hard to believe I was the only one in that state of mind at the time.

I don't even come close to having all the answers to this wonderful chaos of love, light, shadows, stretching, and hope, but I do know there's a Father in heaven who planned and purposed for each and every one of us in this life here on earth.

We all have our own unique parts to play. Not one of us was made the same, and that was very much on purpose, so on a side note, don't try to be someone else, or you may miss the very calling and purpose God specifically made you for.

That's not to say that we have to do XYZ at a certain time or that God can't work without us. He most certainly can and will carry out His plan on earth without us if we choose to not partner with Him.

But He loves us so much that He wants to partner with us and will never stop pursuing us with His love, mercy, and grace.

The only thing that honestly got me out of that dysfunctional, deadly social life that was going around and around in circles was revelation after revelation of God's love and plan and purpose for my life. From the night I found myself lying on the cold tiles of the bathroom floor after a four-day drinking binge over a public holiday, I found myself calling out in desperation to a God I wasn't even sure existed, let alone knowing if He could hear me.

I clearly remember that long weekend. We'd been drinking for four days, day and night. On that fourth night, I remember lying on cold bathroom-floor tiles with my head spinning, and I just blacked out. Although my eyes were wide open, everything was black, and I couldn't see.

I remember tears rolling out and just saying from the very pit of my soul and bottom of my heart, "God, there has got to be more than this. There has got to be more to life than this week in, week out of wasting away."

Nothing magical happened in that moment, and there was no audible voice booming down from heaven telling me what to do, but that day, I made a decision that if indeed there was a God in heaven, He would reach me somehow and wouldn't leave me in a downward spiral anymore. And if He came and met me, I'd give Him a chance.

And there my search to find God began.

I was somewhere between seventeen and eighteen years old, and it was at least six months after that night on the bathroom floor that me and my estranged husband who was my boyfriend at the time were invited to a night service at a local church. When I got there, I thought, *What am I doing? This is not for me*, and I pretty much had a panic attack. I physically couldn't walk in the door. It was at that moment that I had my first encounter with God's peace.

In that moment, my sister, who'd invited us to church, put her hand on my head and prayed. I can't remember what she said. I just remember closing my eyes with tears rolling down my face. I felt so at peace. Then I walked in as if the previous few minutes hadn't even happened.

That night changed my life. It wasn't the songs or the preacher or the people. It was the tangible feeling of God. I didn't understand at the time what it was that I was feeling, but there was this thick atmosphere that no one could come close to creating with people or machines. I knew the God that I was searching for was in that place, and I knew I wanted to meet Him. I just didn't know how.

The following week, we went back to a Sunday morning service and then week after week and message after message. I can't explain what was happening inside, but God was moving in my life and changing me from the inside out. I think it was no more than six months after the first time I stepped foot in the sanctuary that I gave my life to Jesus Christ in the morning service I mentioned earlier.

I don't even remember what the preacher's message was about, as I said, but when he did the altar call, I couldn't keep the tears in, nor could I keep my hand from going up. I'm sure my heart would have leaped out if it could have.

Over the next year, God worked in me and changed me in ways I can't explain. I'd just cry at the back of the main auditorium as I stood in the back row during praise and worship. Every message I heard was on point, as if it were just for me. At this point in my life and journey with God, I knew He was my savior and that my life and purpose was to serve Him and build His church.

Since then, it has been a daily choice to have a relationship with God through prayer and reading my Bible.

Before this moment I had not been able to find what I was searching for because what I was searching for was some kind of "sign" like a fairy godmother with wand waving, magical powers, and fairy dust, or a booming voice from above the clouds. But nothing of the sort happened apart from me making the decision in my heart to honestly, unashamedly opening my heart to have it softened by God, however that was to look.

That sounds all very romantic, doesn't it? But I had no idea back then what I was praying for. If I had known back then that my everyday prayer for God to use me and my life to show all the people around me God's good works, grace, and favor in my life—I'm going to be honest—I probably wouldn't have prayed those prayers.

That's not saying that I'd take back any of the works that God has done in and through me to get me to where I am today, but if I had known the journey and pain I'd have to endure, I'd have been petrified and not accepted it was at all possible to get where I am today. It's almost funny that we pray these prayers, and then God answers them, and we panic at the opportunity He has given us, or it doesn't look like the fairy tale we'd imagined and we say, "This isn't what I wanted! Take it back, God."

But if you're praying big, scary, wild prayers that you think are impossible, then that's exactly where God moves—in the impossible. So watch out!

And if you don't understand how God is even working in the situation you may be finding yourself in right now as you read these words, can I encourage you from personal experience to just keep trusting Him? And in time you will look back as I do now and see how He didn't answer your prayer the way you thought He would, but He actually did it way better than you could have ever planned.

I'm not saying it's going to be easy or smooth sailing, and you may even doubt your trusting abilities, but if you stick with God, you will never ever come second.

I realized before starting this new season of my journey following Jesus that I couldn't understand anything about a God who I didn't even know, a God who everybody else had so much to say about, a God who, to most people I knew—OK, all the people I knew but one—was just some sort of controlling, long-bearded man who sits lazily somewhere on a throne in the clouds, not striking down all the evil-hearted people in this world.

But now that I've seen, now that I've heard, now that I've felt the overwhelming love of God, I will be bold enough to tell you until eternity that if you have these false thoughts of God's character, it's because you don't know God personally. God is love, and so if it's not love you're seeing, it's not from God. If the only Christian friend you have doesn't live a life that paints Jesus as love, then don't go off their bad taste but find out for yourself. I pray that I'd never be that Christian who leaves a bad taste in someone's mouth or taints what God's character really is.

Since I found the love of God that first day to this very day now as I sit here writing, my prayer is that I'd live a life that would show the love of God through me to all those around me and those who know me, that I'd live a life that brings God glory and honor and praise, that people who didn't know Jesus would see Him in my life and come to know Him because there was no other way to explain what was happening in me and through me.

Now that's a very big, bold prayer to pray, and, from what I went through in the past three years to come out the other side, knowing God's name is on the line is both scary and comforting at the same time.

I'm more than confident that God goes before me and behind me and knows how to work all things for my good and that His grace and favor in and over my life would bring him glory, honor, and praise. So in a way, it's all on Him, and I boldly confess that I trust God to finish the good works He started in me, and the same goes for you.

And I am certain that God, who began the good work within you, will continue his work until it is finally finished on the day when Christ Jesus returns. Philippians 1:6

chapter 4

God's Love Is One That Never Fails and Never Runs Out

God is love.

> There is no fear in love, but perfect love casts out fear.
> For fear has to do with punishment, and whoever
> fears has not been perfected in love. 1 John 4:18

There is no fear in love, and when human nature is not familiar with something or someone or the way that something is, we can be filled with fear about that something or someone. Don't get me wrong. God loves people, and He sent His only Son to die for everyone, which includes *you*. So if you find yourself reading this book and you have any thoughts of God's character that don't reflect love, then can I encourage you to dig your feet deeper into a personal relationship with the Holy Spirit and ask him to reveal all the passages about God's love for you?

The Word of God is your weapon and your anchor, so let your roots grow stronger and deeper and your heart be anchored in His love.

Whatever fear you're facing right now, the only thing you need to believe about it is that the Devil is a liar. Fear of any sort doesn't come from God.

> For God did not give us a spirit of timidity or cowardice or fear, but [He has given us a spirit] of power and of love and of sound judgement and personal discipline [abilities that result in a calm, well balanced mind and self-control. 2 Timothy 1:7

Whether it's family being torn apart, relationship issues, sickness, marriage problems, constant worry about your children, fear and anxiety about your past or future, the list of problems in life's journey is endless, but our Father in heaven is greater and bigger than any fear that the Enemy whispers lies about to you.

The enemy is after your heart as well. He is smarter than you think and knows more than we do what's at stake for your heart and destiny, so he'll throw every lie and accusation at you.

A heart change is not overnight. Although you may have seen someone have a breakdown and assume it happened overnight, there would have been warning signs days, weeks, months and even years leading up to the breakdown in that person's heart and mind.

The reason we need to make sure we're choosing to follow Jesus every day is the very same reason the Enemy will try to chip away at your heart every day because if you're not making the daily choices to walk in love, the Enemy tries to mess with your heart and fill it with anger, fear, resentment, bitterness, shame, and guilt, trying to overshadow your hope with hopelessness, helplessness, and worthlessness.

It's simply not enough to think good thoughts all the time. You need to fill yourself with the Word of God so that in these times of doubt or fear we can draw on not only what we feel is good but also what God says about us and the hope we have in Him. His love will never fail us, and His Word will never return void.

So is my word that goes out from my mouth: it will
not return to me empty, but will accomplish what
I desire and achieve the purpose for which I sent it.
Isaiah 55:11

God has started something in you, placed treasure inside of you that only He can pull out. Make a choice today to do something about that and trust Him with all your heart, soul, and mind. He *will* finish what He started in you, His Word says, and it is so.

Before I made the decision to follow Jesus, I thought, like most adults who don't know Jesus, that Christians were nice people but weak, that they needed church to give them hope to keep living because they had no purpose in this life.

I now find that funny because I was quite the hypocrite not being able to find my purpose until I found the love of God. You see, I didn't understand nor had I encounter the love of God, and because I didn't understand, I was scared and on the defensive about church and church people.

Now after more than twelve years on this journey of carrying the cross, I see that being a follower of Jesus is actually one of the hardest daily choices, not because I feel I have to, but because it's easier when circumstances get hard to just run away and remove yourself, to hold grudges, to get bitter and hate people when they have hurt you or judged you time and time again. Don't even get me started on choosing to be selfless instead of selfish.

Maybe it's just me, but even though I knew we were free to make our own choices, although we have a plan and purpose created by God, He will never force us to do anything.

It still took me years to realize I'm the one and only person responsible for my choices and happiness, not my kids, not my spouse, not my parents or brother or sister, not the person I got offended by, and not even God—just me.

In any situation or circumstance, you and only you have the power to make the choice to stay in doubt and misery or the hopeless state you're in. Or you can push in, feel the hurt and pain, and struggle through the change to press on toward Jesus and where He is leading you. One is the easy option that ultimately still leaves you in the misery, which can be extremely tempting because you've been keeping your head afloat for so long already—*What's the difference anyway?* you might think.

I can tell you from my personal experience the easy option is never going to benefit you down the track.

The harder one is probably so unbearable, hence the reason you're still where you are if you feel like you're stuck, but on the other side of the push, His yoke is easy, and His burden is light. On the other side of feeling the hurt and pain is His perfect love and joy, and on the other side of the struggle is a freedom that is unworthy of a word but makes you soar with wings like an eagle every day.

My new saying daily is "no pain, no gain." I couldn't think of a saying with more truth that explains our growth through the seasons we experience. Sometimes your normal might just not be so normal after all. But if it's all you know and have learned, it's going to feel like the hardest thing in the world to change or relearn, but I can tell you a hundred percent it's worth the pain to change.

Imagine as an adult trying to relearn what love, patience, kindness, self-control, joy, and gentleness is. It's not going to be easy, and the struggle is real.

I always say that you don't realize how selfish you are until you get married. Then you can't believe you still had selfishness in you once you have a baby. But just wait until the second child comes and you're in disbelief you even had two minutes to think about yourself in a day, but there you find yourself, with room to still somehow be selfish.

Ok, maybe I'm just preaching to myself here but honestly choosing every day to follow God's plan and purpose for my life, while choosing to try and grow and be more like Jesus every day is the biggest most important decision I have to make every morning when I wake up.

Don't get me wrong. I wouldn't change the life I get to live for the world, but I just want get the point across that someone who's choosing to follow Jesus and who has a heart after God's own is one of the bravest, strongest, and most courageous people on earth.

I have learned that following Jesus means giving up everything that separates you from God to do the will of God. Now that doesn't mean to quit your job, sell your house, car, and all your belongings, and volunteer at your local church full time—unless you really are called to do that. It means to put God first in everything, including your current job or whatever is in your hand, and working at it as if it was unto God.

You'll never come second by putting God first. I've said it before, and I'll say it a thousand times more. That isn't some pretty little cliché saying either. If anyone asks me for advice on life choices, it's always my first piece to give, and from my own experience in life, it's the real deal.

I know this from experience time and time again. Most of the time, it doesn't make sense, but those times I chose to put Him first when it didn't make sense have probably been the times when I have needed to really dig deep into His Word and remind myself of all His promises and that He is a good Father. Although I may not understand at the time, He wants what is not just good for me but what is best for me. And He knows what that is.

> Which of you, if your son asks for bread, will give him a stone? Or if he asks for a fish, will give him a snake? If you, then, though are evil, know how to give good gifts to those who ask him! Matthew 7:9–11

I bet you have heard this said from the platform at a church service or read in a verse from the Bible at least: love God with all your heart and love people.

If you're anything like I was before I met Jesus and even as a new Christian, I disliked people, and really, I mean I disliked a lot of people. I found it hard to trust and let friends in or get close, although I didn't know then when I was in the middle of it that I was just afraid of being hurt.

My easy option was just to not like them. To be honest, I even found it hard to like people, let alone love them, when I was a new Christian. Especially when everyone was so nice at church, it was easy to be suspicious because my normal was that if someone was that nice, they wanted something from me unless they were my immediate family.

I went on my own journey seeking after God's own heart and finding His love and heart for all people, even if I had labeled them unworthy in my eyes. The revelation I got was that I myself was not worthy, but by the grace of God, He still saved a wretch like me. I found it a lot easier to love people when I started to love God with all my heart first.

> And he said to him, "You shall love The Lord your
> God with all your heart and with all your souls and
> with all your mind. This is the greatest and first
> commandment. And a second is like it: You shall
> love your neighbor as yourself." Matthew 22:37–39

In another translation, the message says, "Love others as well as you love yourself." If you don't have love in you, that explains why you can't love others. Others are basically everyone else in the world that's not you, even the people you really dislike.

There was so much dysfunction in my estranged husband's family that it made me feel as if my family was normal and just like all families, mine is not "normal". Even reality tv families you've watched on TV would have seemed normal.

Yet I still chose to love them, even when he professed his hatred and disgust for his own family. At most times, I agreed with him, but I still encouraged him to love them. There are adults that love and cherish children, who will raise them to flourish in life, knowing they're sending them out to be functioning adults into the world. And there are adults who use children as accessories and have ownership over them, thinking that because they were part of physically making them that the children are "theirs."

I think that the more we realize the children we're raising up as the next generation aren't ours but God's children whom He has entrusted us with, the more our eyes are opened to the responsibility of what parenting really is.

If I was ever steering my children into the grave, I pray someone in my life would speak life and wisdom into my situation. A child is a treasure you've been entrusted with, and don't ever forget that. I think if more people saw it that way, maybe there wouldn't be so much judgment on moms who pause their corporate careers to do one of the most important jobs in the world—raising the next generation.

Don't get me wrong. Some moms can work full time outside the home and still raise amazing young people, but it's not just feeding them morning, midday, and night and expecting them to grow. They'd have a mentor other than yourself that they would be leaning and gleaning from as they spent time with them if you were out of the home. Again, I need to say that there's nothing wrong with that. Have you ever heard the saying "it takes a village to raise a child"? Well, if you haven't, then you have now. And that is one village per child. I know from experience. HA!

It's important to know that whoever kids are spending time with the most is who they're learning from the most. It's not necessarily the words they speak. It's also the mannerisms, the way they walk, the way they talk and carry themselves. All this is learned not from a textbook or being told how to—it's learned when small children watch and absorb without even knowing it.

Some people reading this may not agree with me or like this next part, but I strongly believe that if a child is in an unstable home or in a home experiencing any type of domestic violence, then they aren't going to thrive as they should in childhood or life if they weren't in that environment. Like a desert plant is not going to flourish in a tropical environment, and a tropical plant is not going to flourish in a desert, they will slowly rot away or dry out.

I don't know how I can sensitively put this into words that won't offend anyone, but growing up in an unhealthy environment can be exactly what can obscure a child's mind and lead to them being dysfunctional teenagers, which can then lead to being very unhealthy adults. And then possibly the cycle begins. Unless chains are broken in the adult, it keeps going around in the family circle.

It doesn't have to be this way, and it isn't supposed to be this way. God created family. It's His masterpiece in creation that represents and reveals His character through us and our families.

God has this unending love that He can reveal and shine through family, and that's why I believe the Enemy loves to try to separate and divide families.

> Two are better than one, because they have a good return for their labor: if either of them falls down, one can help the other up. But pity anyone who falls and has no one to help them up. Also if two lie down together, they will keep warm. But how can one keep warm alone? Though one may be overpowered, two can defend themselves. A cord of three strands is not quickly broken. Ecclesiastes 4:9–12

The Devil wants nothing more than to break down relationships because he knows just as much as we do that there's power when we take a stand together as believers. Jesus even tells us this.

> For where two or three gather in my name, there am I with them. Matthew 18:20

Although I knew this everyday fight was spiritual, there was a time when I let the Enemy dull that knowledge in my mind, and because I didn't face it for what it was, I just let it get me down.

As a younger girl and an immature follower of Jesus, I put up with things I was meant to conquer. I have been following Jesus for over twelve years now, but to be honest, it has only been the last three years that I've been calling the Enemy out boldly for his lies and schemes.

The enemy might sound like a roaring lion, but don't forget he's not the lion, hence the reason scripture says the Enemy goes around roaring *like* a lion because he is just an imposter trying to move our focus off Jesus and onto fear.

Journeying through an emotional abusive relationship full of lies, infidelity, and anger issues, it would be so easy to blame my estranged husband for the waves of turmoil, pain, debt, and everything else that came with being left feeling raw, abandoned, and not good enough. But I knew I couldn't drown in the sorrow and fear that the Enemy tried to flush me out with.

It was in those moments that I found myself on my knees in the bathroom crying, trying to hide my pain from my children. One moment I was getting mad and asking God endless questions and demanding answers, begging God to tell me why and asking Him what I was supposed to do. The next moment, I was only able to make groaning noises because I had no tears left, let alone the physical strength to pull myself together and get off the floor.

But in my weakest and most broken moments when I felt as if I'd come to the end of my rope of hope, God would very gently scoop me up and remind me that He will never give me more than I can actually handle, and His peace would fall. In those desperate moments when I couldn't bear any more, He offered a way out through His perfect peace that surpassed all understanding. If I understood, then it wouldn't be peace that surpassed understanding. I feel that for someone who is searching and begging God for an answer, the fact that you don't understand is the golden ticket to receiving that peace from Him. Be still and know that He is God and He works *all* things together for those who love him. Trust him. God's word doesn't fail, and He is not a man that would lie. You need to get that down deep in your spirit and tell your soul that God is trustworthy.

I might add to that God never scooped me up and out, and it wasn't a magical moment removed of emotion and pain. But I knew His presence was with me to walk me through the fire, and my hope and faith in God would have another layer added. I'm not going to lie, so many times I wanted God to pick me up and take me out, not walk through with me. But ultimately I knew that if I didn't go through this time, it would only be harder the next time around.

One thing I've learned over the years is that God will give us unending chances and will never give up on us, but if we try to do it our own way, it's just not going to work out.

God has this never-ending love for you, and I pray that if anything jumps out from these pages and into your heart, it's that God *is* love, and He is *for* you. No matter what the Enemy throws your way and no matter who he uses, God's love for you is greater and stronger. It will break every chain and oppression over your life.

Maybe nothing I or anyone else can say will raise your hope that you'll make it through, so I encourage you to read these verses that I confessed over the days when I felt too weak to even speak. I pray that God will encourage you and spur that hope to rise within you. Open your heart and mouth to Jesus and wait on Him.

> When you pass through the waters, I will be with you; and when you pass through the rivers, they will not sweep over you. When you walk through the fire, you will not be burned; the flames will not set you ablaze. Isaiah 43:2

> So do not fear, for I am with you; do not be dismayed, for I am your God. I will strengthen you

and help you; I will uphold you with my righteous right hand. Isaiah 41:10

Have I not commanded you? Be strong and courageous. Do not be afraid; do not be discouraged, for the Lord your God will be with you wherever you go." Joshua 1:9

For the Spirit God gave us does not make us timid, but gives us power, love and self-discipline. 2 Timothy 1:7

Cast all your anxiety on him because he cares for you. 1 Peter 5:7

The name of the Lord is a fortified tower; the righteous run to it and are safe.
Proverbs 18:10

My comfort in my suffering is this: Your promise preserves my life. Psalm 119:50

Be strong and take heart, all you who hope in the Lord. Psalm 31:24

I have told you these things, so that in me you may have peace. In this world you will have trouble. But take heart! I have overcome the world." John 16:33

Trust in the Lord with all your heart and lean not on your own understanding; in all your ways submit to him, and he will make your paths straight. Proverbs 3:5–6

Praise to the God of All Comfort

Praise be to the God and Father of our Lord Jesus
Christ, the Father of compassion and the God of
all comfort, who comforts us in all our troubles, so
that we can comfort those in any trouble with the
comfort we ourselves receive from God.
2 Corinthians 1:3–4

Peace I leave with you; my peace I give you. I do
not give to you as the world gives. Do not let your
hearts be troubled and do not be afraid. John 14:27

I shared earlier that I learned in the past two years to call out
the Enemy at his plans and schemes. When I learned to notice the
patterns and prepare myself for the ultimate battle, with prayer and
the Word of God, what was revealed was more than I thought was
ever possible.

I prayed dangerous prayers for my then husband, prayers for
freedom, healing from brokenness, and that God would use all
that the Enemy was doing and turn it to good, that God would be
glorified in the miraculous turnaround, that whatever darkness my
spouse was going through he would come out of the fire refined as
pure gold is and not one smell of smoke would be evident on him.
I had prayers that I wrote out and stuck all over the back on my
ensuite door that I prayed every day.

No prayer goes unanswered, but sometimes they just don't get
answered the way we thought. My prayers for freedom, healing,
refining, and coming out without a smell of smoke did get answered,
beyond what I even thought was possible. But it was me who was
refined, set free, and healed, and the kids and I came through the
fire without smelling of smoke.

At the very end of December 2015, I had a vision of a single,
white flower shooting up in the desert. It was thriving in the midst

of nothing with a cracked desert ground surrounding it. Then a few weeks later, I had a dream of a white dandelion blowing around in the wind but not losing a single seed.

I told a close friend of mine over lunch, and I asked her, "What do you think it means?" We discussed flowers, God, and what we understood the meaning could be, and we concluded it could be like a new beginning and a new life, like a new flower sprouting.

I was convinced it was for whatever my estranged husband was going through that God would soften his heart, change and mold him to the mighty man of God he was called to be.

But I should have known better, and I remembered that every time I'd prayed prayers like that for people in my life that I'd wanted to change, God had worked and changed me not them.

A few months later, I was attending a women's conference where God literally spoke to me in every single session. I was still very raw, coming to terms with a lot of the realities I was facing, like going through a divorce and dealing with the issues from all the years past. On top of that, I was trying to stay on top of my own thoughts about myself and what God thought and said about me instead of the rejection I had faced.

I was so blessed I had two very dear, sweet friends who looked after me the entire conference, which included having the same seats at every session. You may be thinking, *Why would you mention something so insignificant?* This random bit of information is important to know for one reason, not because it meant I had my name on a chair, although that in itself was significant, God whispered to me from night one, *"You were meant to be here. This very seat has your name on it because you belong here right in this very moment."*

The quick work that I thought God was going to do in my estranged husband was actually a quick work in me. Understand this: a quick work doesn't necessarily mean God changes your circumstances and removes all the obstacles and mountains in an instant, although He could and He has done that in many situations in people's lives. But know that most work God does is on the inside where you can't even see.

Sometimes God doesn't take you out of the situation because He's using it to do a quick work inside you, and by the time you come out the other side of that circumstance (and you will come out), you'll look back and see how not only did God show up every step of the way and not only did you come out restored, receiving a double portion back of everything the Enemy stole from you, but that very circumstance that you thought was your biggest challenge ended up being the biggest change you made in your life, in your sphere, in your family, in your workplace, or in the world so far in your life.

The timeline of what God had been doing in my life and speaking to me about in the two-year lead-up to this point was that I wasn't as alone as I felt. God really had gone before and behind me and my children.

On the final day of the conference in the very last session, our seats that we'd sat every session for three days were moved from the right side of the stage to the front and center of the stage. At the time, it didn't mean much apart from having a full view of the stage from left to right (which was pretty spectacular), but then it happened—God sealed the deal over my heart with all that He had spoken to me about throughout the conference.

There it was, right in front of my face, the dandelion-looking flower from my dream months earlier.

One of the flowers popped up on the left and right side of stage and then began to twirl.

At first, I thought, *Wow, God you're so hilarious!*

But the laughter soon turned into a flowing river of tears as a water fountain dropped from the middle of the stage, meters from my face, the words written with lights shining through the water:

Go home, flourish, and tell of His great love.

It was in that exact moment that the Holy Spirit whispered to me that the flower was me all along.

I felt a warm embrace from behind my shoulders, and I felt my heavenly Father's love overwhelm my soul as the Holy Spirit whispered to me, *"You don't have to have it under control* because *I do."* I embraced that moment and let out a sob when I turned around to receive the embrace from my friend who I thought was putting her arms around me. She wasn't behind me. She was next to me, and my legs were pressed against the chair. I realized that only the chair was behind me.

It is moments like these that no one can take away from you. Moments like these that mark you. They make the whole world stop and stand still around you as God wraps His love around your heart and your soul declares that God is good, kind, gracious, and loving. It's almost unexplainable in words, that moment when you get a fresh revelation or God speaks to you.

When I was a new Christian, I used to think God would never speak directly to me. He was obviously too busy doing things God does, whatever it was I thought God did. Funny, you may think, but I bet there's someone else out there who has thought something along those lines: "He's too busy" or "I'm too insignificant to have a direct line to God."

Here's the problem with that kind of thought: the Devil is a liar, and what more would he love than for you to think that God is too busy to think about you? The Bible tells us God hears our prayers and knows what we need before we even ask.

> But when you pray, go into your room, close the door and pray to your Father, who is unseen. Then your Father, who sees what is done in secret, will reward you. And when you pray, do not keep on babbling like pagans, for they think they will be heard because of their many words. Do not be like

them, for your Father knows what you need before you ask him. Matthew 6:6–13

Let me remind you now not only that God's thoughts about you are more than you could imagine, but also that He knows you inside out, and you're more than precious to Him. Remind yourself of that every day, speak it out loud, read it to yourself in the mirror every morning when you wake up, and watch the Enemy flee.

For you created my inmost being; you knit me together in my mother's womb. I praise you because I am fearfully and wonderfully made; your works are wonderful, I know that full well. My frame was not hidden from you when I was made in the secret place, when I was woven together in the depths of the earth. Your eyes saw my unformed body; all the days ordained for me were written in your book before one of them came to be. How precious to me are your thoughts, God! How vast is the sum of them! Were I to count them, they would outnumber the grains of sand when I awake, I am still with you. Psalm 139:13–18

I faced a reality that even though God was moving and working in my life and my children's lives, it seemed to be getting worse with my estranged husband at the time, and each day I went deeper with God seemed to mean that what started off with him saying in his own words " he was not being able to stand me," led him to become bitter and full of hatred toward me and how I felt about Jesus.

I had the revelation that the very reason God gives us free will to choose is because He loves us. If He took our ability to choose and controlled our thoughts, actions, or our free will to follow or not follow Him, then that would mean God wouldn't love us. But as it stands, God is love, so we'll always have free will to follow or not follow.

No matter how much or how many people I had praying for my estranged husband, if he was ultimately not choosing to let God back into his life, God would never force His way back in. That was the choice he had made, which led him down three years of choices that turned him not just into a stranger but into someone who was so destructive and damaging that I had to lean into no one else but God to draw the line of where it all stops.

Divorce was never an option or even a word we used, so I went into panic mode even having to think about that process and what it meant for me and the kids. I hadn't even experienced divorce in my immediate family.

I got to the point of thinking everyone I knew or who knew me would be judging me, thinking, *What's wrong with her that he didn't want her anymore?*

Now you tell me who would even believe that kind of ridiculous lie, right? Well, I did, for weeks and probably even months, I battled with so much shame and had to put into serious practice capturing every thought and reminding myself hourly of exactly what God says about me.

I had to remind myself that as much as I was told by him that it was all me and there was nothing wrong with him, actually, no, it wasn't about me—it was about him. There was a list of lies that tried daily to get a foothold in my head:

> You cannot be a solo mom in ministry.
> You can no longer give people advice on marriage
> or relationships if they come to you.
> You cannot lead a team while you're going through
> a divorce.
> Your team won't even trust you anymore.
> You can no longer sit in the front with the rest of
> the pastors.

You actually aren't good enough.

You can no longer pray for people because you need prayer and healing first.

You cannot be this free and full of you still—you must be cold hearted.

You probably aren't that pretty, you know.

You cannot trust anyone that's what got you in this mess to start with.

You must be stupid to be so trustworthy.

What will people think about me getting divorced?

What will people think is wrong with me?

That's not even half the lies and questions I battled with every day, and if any of these resonate with you for more than a split second, catch it, call it out for the lie it is, open your Bible, and search for the truth of what God says in your situation to you. So many times, we text or call our best friends, mentors, or someone trustworthy in our lives to ask for their advice on what to do. And that's OK; we should seek wise counsel. *But* can I remind you of the book that is our cheat sheet to life. There is a word for every season, every trial, and every situation you can go through in this life.

God's word is sharper than a double-edged sword. Do you understand what that means? No matter what happens to us, or what's said about us, or what's even said to us, no matter how much it hurts like a dagger in the stomach or the heart, you can take the Word of God in every situation possible and cut the Devil right back!

I had to remind my self daily that it's not over and God wants to work in and through me on this season in life, when the thoughts crept in that I wasn't good enough and maybe I just deserved all this, maybe I should pack up, leave and try to start afresh, whatever that means (aka running away and not dealing with your baggage).

I learned to not trust my feelings but only the facts. Feelings aren't bad—God made us with feelings after all—but you can never make life-changing decisions based on your feelings and emotions.

You must clear your head from your emotions and deal with the facts.

It only took me twenty-eight years of doing life to get this revelation, but it was better late than never!

The feelings and emotions would just overwhelm me and get me in a pattern where the Enemy had a good foothold to steal my joy. When I finally learned this, I'd call the Enemy out and say out loud, *"You cannot have my joy because my joy comes from the Lord!"*

I truly believe there is power in speaking truth and speaking it out load. So many times, I found myself stomping around my home, pointing my finger in the air and declaring the good things God has already done in my life and the kids' lives, calling the Enemy out on his whispering, cowering lies.

The biggest one was letting the Enemy know that I knew his plans, and I knew my estranged spouse was not the Enemy: *"But you are, Devil, and you cannot touch me or my children because we're children of God."*

Declaring truth always cleared my head from emotions, and that's when the facts would start pouring in and the Holy Spirit would remind me of truth and convictions. This is why it's so important we dwell in His word so that in these moments the Holy Spirit can remind us of what we know.

It's as simple as this: if it's not in us, then it won't come out, so we need to continually fill ourselves with the Word of God, not because it's a daily ritual and we have to, but because it's the weapon God Himself has given us to use against the Enemy. The Word of God is the double-edged sword that cuts through anything the Enemy could attempt to drag us down or bind us up with. I have to remind myself weekly that I may have to fight some battles, and some over and over again, but here's the good news, and it's your good news too:

The war has been won by Jesus already.

You probably know this verse well, but Jesus says we will have troubles to face but He follows on to say take heart I have overcome the world!

> I have told you these things, so that in me you may
> have peace. In this world you will have trouble. But
> take heart! I have overcome the world. John 16:33

Hurt people hurt people. It's something I had heard a lot in life, but to be honest, I thought it was just a catch phrase. Definitely never did I ever think the man I loved and was devoted to with my whole heart would betray and hurt me to what I thought at the time was damage beyond repair inside of me.

I was told I was never loved at all, that he couldn't stand me or anything about me, that in the thirteen years we were together he'd never enjoyed any of it, not one single day. He told the children he never loved me, and it was my fault that he left. They were devastated and confused to say the least, and that broke my heart all over again.

Emotions would get the better of me in the moments the kids would share comments with me that they had heard or been told by a person they should have been able to trust wholeheartedly, their dad. Emotion would get me nowhere but in a messy bundle of tears and sorrow with a burning hole in my chest of fiery pain.

Why do I share what I just shared, you may ask. It's only just a scratch of the surface of what I had to unwillingly journey through, and I thought long, hard, and deep about sharing any of those parts of my story because I want to share a reality that I don't think gets shared. I think we cover things up in shame maybe or maybe even because we just don't know how, but one of the very reasons I never asked for help or talked to anyone about what happened behind closed doors was because no one talked about these kinds of things.

Sometimes in moments like this, there's no person you can go to for comfort or advice, no mother, no pastor, no best friend, and no counselor, but I learned quickly that I needed to take my business directly to my Father in heaven and deal directly with Him.

I was my children's safe place, and just like they were coming to me with what they felt upset about, I went straight to my Father in heaven because I knew He was the one I could go to and He'd listen and see my heart, catch my tears, and love me through it. I didn't know anything else beyond that, but just like my children's instinct was to go to their mother, mine was to go to my Father.

I pray that however you may find yourself reading this, for whatever reason, if you don't think you can run to God for safety, would you receive this revelation and know that God sees you, He sees your heart, He sees your tears, He sees your pain, He sees your hurt, He sees your struggle, He sees the mess, He sees your soul, your innermost being because He made you, He purposed for your very life, and He saw it all.

I know you may not understand right now if you're in a moment of your life where there's deep pain and hurt beyond words can describe. If you can't see beyond the pain and struggle, take these words to heart. And don't trust me, but as I testify in hope to encourage you that you can trust in our Father who has promised to prosper you beyond your wildest imagination.

It may not be in the way you thought your life would be right now, and it might take longer than you pray for, but God will finish the good work He has started in you, and if you trust Him with your innermost being, the innermost being that He created, then I'm convinced you'll see the good works overflowing beyond your own life and into those all around you.

> Being confident of this very thing, that He who has begun a good work in you will complete it until the day of Jesus Christ. Philippians 1:6

The Lord will fulfill his purpose for me; your steadfast love, O Lord, endures forever. Do not forsake the work of your hands. Psalm 138:8

God can take my tears, my pain, my hurt, my anger and if I'm going to point my finger and get real mad at him with all my "why-God-whys"! he can take that too. Who better to go to for a big cry and soul pour out, who better understands our hearts, than the Father who created our innermost beings?

Here is the tricky part. I can stay in the hurt and pain, and wallow in the misery of my situation that I had, or I can trust God and live a life that honors him and move on.

Year after year and season after season, if I look back, there were alarm bells and warning signs or whatever you want to call them that I was in an unhealthy relationship, i said it earlier but the fact is that hurt people hurt people.

Once I had realized that part, by getting professional help from counseling and psychologists, I began to have parts of my heart open to God that I didn't even realize were not open to Him already. I received the revelation of how wide and deep God's love for me really was, the love that never runs out, that is bigger and covers over any hurt that anyone can do or try to do to me.

Can I encourage you, if you have been in a damaging relationship of any kind or maybe you think you are or have been but you're not sure because nothing is normal for you, then reach out to a safe person or organization in your area?

God's love never fails.

chapter 5

If God Is Love, Then Love Is the Key

Raise your hand if you're someone who won't stop until you get what you want! Hold up. You didn't raise your hand. And neither did I, I thought, until I realized I've stopped typing because I have raised both my hands, one for me and one for you because I realized that no one can pursue like I can when I want something. And I have a feeling I may not be the only one.

Now, I'm not talking about the screaming child who wants every toy on the shelf of the toy aisle that you just run past as fast as you can, as though you were being chased by an assassin, to the checkout line.

Because every time you're in the mall, your child and every other child is grabbing for toys, left, right, and center, throwing them in your shopping cart even after you have explained to them for the fifteenth time, "It's not your birthday, my sweet child. We're shopping for your friend's birthday present."

What about the teenager who wants to hang out with "that" friend or sleep over on a school night and won't stop asking and arguing with you. They always ask at the most inconvenient times, in hopes that you'll just brush them off, saying, "Yes, OK, just make sure you do your homework," or, "Make sure you clean your room before you go," or, "Make sure you—" You counter with something they need to make sure of so that you're also getting your own way— ha! I know this from personal experience when I was a teenager and now a mom of two very savvy kids who can talk back.

Come on, guys. We've all been in a moment like that child, or we have a child who'll pursue something insignificant and do everything possible to make sure they get their way.

Can you make the decision and commitment to pursue God that same way?

The choice is yours to make. You actually don't have to, but if you choose not to, you're missing out. I know you may not be able to see how, but let me tell you a story of the impossible and unbearable choice of choosing to pursue love and why I say you're missing out if you choose not to pursue.

Going way back to when I was only fifteen years old, I thought I'd found the love of my life. I made a choice then as a broken, needy young teen to find my other half in someone else, to fill a hole in my heart and the gap in my life that I thought belonged to another person.

Let me pause there for a minute and just bring you a big dose of reality if we aren't on the same page. No one—and I mean no one, not your spouse, the person you're longing for to marry one day, any member of your family, your best friend, or even your beloved child—can complete you or be your other half. It's a lovely line you may hear at a wedding that "you complete me" or "two have become one and are now complete."

Dear sweet one reading this, let me tell you if no one has: you were complete when God made you and called you by name. There may be a longing or void in your life, but ain't no man, woman, or child going to fill that void in your heart and soul.

God made that space inside of you along with every other imperfect but perfect part of your body, and He can fit perfectly in that space. I say all that bluntly, not with bitterness or anger but with a complete confidence and a revelation that we have spouses, children, friends, and family to make this journey with, but they in no way complete us.

We were made for relationships, and we need relationships in our lives—don't get me wrong. And, oh, what a powerful force it is when we gather as family in the purpose of God's will on this earth.

Don't ever live a second of your life thinking you're missing out on something or that you're incomplete because you may not have that "other half" or have yet birthed that child you're longing to do the journey with.

When I was a young teenager and I'd found that person that I thought completed me, I was all in. I was committed to the very end, till death do us part, ride or die, to never turning back no matter what, to be defending and protecting, possibly smothering, and loving till the ends of the earth. If you know me or ask my close friends, you'll know that the way I love is mafia style: once you're in with me and have my heart, you're in, and there's no turning back on my behalf.

I pursued, protected, and defended like I was throwing punches to win the title. No matter what my family or friends (who loved me with their whole hearts) had to say about the toxic behaviour i was getting myself into, I had a defense for my estranged spouse's unhealthy behavior and reactions. I loved him beyond the way a girlfriend should and, now that I look back, probably loved on him like a mother would her child as well.

Was all this helpful? Probably not because he needed to grow up and learn how to be a mature functioning adult himself and there was nothing I could do to teach him that, although I tried.

I'm not going to pretend I was Miss Perfect. I felt as if I was failing and falling fast down into a deep, dark hole, while trying to do everything I could to help a broken, shattered little boy inside a teenager's body, yet I was a broken teenager girl myself.

Fast-forward through a lot of unhealthy, bad behavior, bad

choices, and shame behind closed doors, we were invited to a church, and we both accepted Jesus. Or so I thought we both did.

In the next few years, we got married. I wasn't only radically saved and renewed but being transformed from the inside out on a rate so fast I could barely keep up with myself and who I used to be. All the past was being left way behind, and I felt as if a brand-new person every day, loving life, having found this new love in my life, this real God who I'd always seemed to long for deep down inside for as a long as I can remember, even as a small child.

After about three years of following Jesus, I went into full-time ministry, and every day I was changing and growing at a rate I thought was on the same page as my then husband. He was serving in his gifting and in his element—so it looked on the outside. He made a few friends, and he was coming to events and social hangouts when he wasn't working.

God's hand was so evident on our lives, from the smallest to the tallest of things. Like the week I left the corporate world and started in full-time ministry he received a pay raise the same amount I took a pay cut. God always showed up financially every time I put Him first, from the first time we moved into a rental together to new jobs and pay raises, buying our first apartment, the list goes on, but God showed up with His favor and blessing every single time.

There was always some tension between my generosity versus my estranged husband's, but again, I had an excuse from his past that justified his thoughts, though they didn't align with the Word on sacrifices financially or be it time and effort to build God's house, give to missions, or being generous to others in need.

I do remember longing for him to lead us the way I saw other godly men leading their families or wanting him to encourage me the way other husbands I saw encourage their wives, but one thing I still had from my past wasn't just a bag, but an eighty-pound suitcase full of excuses and defenses for him and his behavior in every situation or circumstance.

Fast-forward another six or seven years, and we started a family after being told by doctors I couldn't start a family naturally. It was a miracle. I didn't only birth one child but two stunning little treasures from heaven. Now, have you ever heard or seen the hashtag *LTD*? That was my life on the outside, *living the dream*.

But on the inside, it was this moment in my personal journey that I think reality was trying to tell me something wasn't right. In fact, something was wrong, very wrong, and I tried to ignore it. I ignored my family around me. I hid the shame from my friends. I prayed and cried. And most times I just silently wept to God because He was the only safe place I knew I could say what I needed to say and ask what I needed to ask because I knew He saw my heart and He knew before I even asked or said what I was going to say anyway.

I didn't understand what exactly was happening in my life and why, but I thought it was going to be like this forever, so I had just settled to the living conditions, although deep down I knew it wasn't right for life and family to be like this. But I couldn't see how it would or could ever change. I had tried get professional help, but he wasn't willing. I knew this was not what God had for us.

God's promises for us are a life better than we could ever imagine and one of abundance.

> But, as it is written, "What no eye has seen, nor ear heard, nor the heart of man imagined, what God has prepared for those who love him." 1 Corinthians 2:9

> Now to him who is able to do far more abundantly than all that we ask or think, according to the power at work within us. Ephesians 3:20

Major childhood issues started to arise that were never dealt with, and my estranged husband insisted that he didn't have a problem because he didn't do the specific actions of violence to me and the kids that had been done to him or that he'd seen as a child. At the time I was stuck in the middle of thirteen years of emotional abuse that had shaped me and what I ultimately thought about myself from the core of my being as a fifteen-year-old girl to a twenty-seven-year-old mother and wife. Even though I knew what God said about me, what my estranged husband said about me was louder.

I constantly made the *choice* to find God in the mix of my life and to always run back to His presence, His promise, and His word. As part of human nature, I think we always go back to what we know, but sometimes, unfortunately, for some it's not God they run back to. It's the dysfunction they knew as their "normal" from a child or possibly drugs and alcohol to numb the pain of the words and world as a teen or adult.

For some, when they've encountered Jesus they cannot ever shake the power of His presence and love in their lives, so they don't just go back to it—they run and pursue it like children who have fallen facedown flat at the park running back to their moms, hysterically crying in pain.

I see myself over the last two years running back to my heavenly Father, crying hysterically, face drooping, full of pain so bad it burned in my chest, made me sick to my stomach, and, at too many times to count, had me buckled at the knees, crying on the bathroom floor.

Some moments, only tears would fall, and I hoped desperately in my heart God was there to catch them because I could barely speak, let alone pray. Sometimes crying wasn't even an option because the pain was too much to bear, and only moans of despair were released as my heart just cried out to God. Inside, I'd scream, *This is too much! I cannot do this anymore! I have nothing left! You said you would never give me more than I could bear.*

Can I tell you that in every single one of these moments of deep despair, it was there, that what was within me is what came out. it was God's word that would gently seep out like a warm memory and cover my mind.

Oh, the times I found myself in that situation in life and say how I wish that Jesus would have physically appeared and scooped me into His arms to carry my raw, hurting, emotional flesh into another world other than the one I was lying in on the bathroom floor, but then every time I look back, I see how God's love surrounded me and gave me the strength to somehow carry on.

I'm grateful he loves us enough to strengthen us and not just scoop us up and carry us away without growing or learning more about His perfect love for us.

Remind yourself daily that He is a good God and knows what's best for us.

As I mentioned earlier, He reminded me that He had not left me every single time I found myself in that big black hole of death and defeat. He was with me, and He would bring me back to the reality of knowing it's not actually about me.

Ouch, now that I type that out I can see that even when I was in my greatest moments of despair I was in a small little bubble world, asking, "What about me?"

> The Lord is my light and my salvation; whom shall
> I fear? The Lord is the strength of my life; of whom
> shall I be afraid? Psalm 27:1

> But the salvation of the righteous is from the Lord;
> He is their strength in time of trouble. Psalm 37:39

> In the day when I cried out, you answered me,
> And made me bold with your strength in my soul.
> Psalm 138:3

> I can do all things through Christ who strengthens
> me. Philippians 4:13

I can choose to love the very people who have hurt and betrayed me, one of whom was my husband at the time with whom I was sharing for half of my life time literally. A husband or wife is the person you're supposed to love and trust the most out of every other human being in the world, the person who you hang on every word and believe what they said about you. Your story may be different than mine, but if it's similar and someone you loved hurt you so much the pain was unbearable to the point that you're searching the world for hope you'll make it through this, then I'm writing this for you.

Listen to me and listen carefully. My pain wasn't wasted. God's love for me is so real. No one can take that away from me, and that same love that covered me covers you. In His perfect timing, God will bring you through what you think you're currently stuck in.

Don't get comfortable in the valley. Pack up your tent and belongings and get ready to start climbing your mountain with Jesus! He'll be right there with you. He's already one step in front of you with His hand stretched out, waiting for you to take the first step.

God will give you strength, grace, and all you need grow to handle your situation. It doesn't mean you forget what someone may have said or done to you, but it means that although you know it's wrong, it's not going to hold you down in bitterness, hatred, toil, and turmoil because it's Christ in you who gives you the strength, and you're not alone.

Your head will probably tell you that you're alone and you need to protect yourself. Or maybe to keep up your guard and don't let it go! If you let it go, you're weak. But that's a lie. You're stronger than you know and most definitely stronger for choosing to love instead of hate.

You may say, how can you say that? You have no idea what happened to me or was said to me and about me and how that affected me. You're right. I have no idea. But what I do know is that I had to choose to obey God and love my neighbor, and I came to terms with the fact that I actually couldn't do it by myself in my own will.

I couldn't get past my estranged husband's voice and his words: "I hate you. There is nothing I like about you. I never loved you."

Now, that's the PG version. It was beyond wrong, and the Enemy had me thinking that I deserved it somehow as I would sit there with tears streaming down my face not knowing where to look and wondering if i could try muster up the emotional energy to ask him why he is saying all of that.

You see, on the outside I looked confident, loud, and outgoing, but on the inside, I was so insecure I couldn't even meet new people, and I found it extremely hard to make friends. It took me weeks of praying and fasting to rid my heart and soul of any trace of bitterness and hatred, but ultimately, it was me doing my own business with God.

There was a moment that I went from a burning hatred in my stomach and a fiery urge for revenge to crying tears for my estranged husband's soul. It wasn't a feeling of superiority or pity on him, but a genuine prayer and feeling of urgency for his soul to come back to Jesus. The hate and bitterness that began to creep in was taken away and later changed to genuine forgiveness. *Only* God can do that in your life; it's actually impossible to try on your own.

I remember it was my birthday, and I had gone into the office to see one of my best friends, and as I walked through, I passed another friend who is a life long friend to my destiny but also a friend who had been on the journey of my husband leaving me for no apparent reason several times over the span of a year. We didn't surround our conversations with updates of how things were going, so it had been over two weeks since we'd talked about the most recent findings in the mystery of him leaving, which was, on top of everything else, his infidelity.

She asked me how I was doing. Usually there would be a pause when asked that question so my mind could catch up with who I actually was having a conversation with and what I wanted to reveal with them in my raw state at the time, but there was no hesitation, and I just let it straight out to her, "You know what? I genuinely feel sorry for him, and if I saw him from afar, I think I'd just see his soul and feel sorry for him." It was followed by a wow response, but then she said what I already knew to be true: "That's God's work."

I tell you this because it was God. I don't want to toot my own horn but loudly toot His, not that God needs a horn, but I cannot even put into words how God can change you and set you free from things that aren't even your own doing. That week was the week I was set free and literally free indeed. It was like a weight had been lifted off. No words can adequately explain the physical feeling of freedom.

> But Jesus looked at them and said to them, with
> men this is impossible, but with God all things are
> possible. Matthew 19:26

Did I know the kind of possible things God was going to do with me, my kids, and my situation? Absolutely no idea! But I know He has gone before and behind us and has a way of using the very thing that tried to destroy you to restore you.

I clung to Matthew 19:26 from the start of what I thought was my life as I knew it being over. I prayed and spoke this verse too many times to count. I prayed for the impossible to happen over my husband at the time who was running from God, our marriage, and down the path of destruction.

I was convinced my faith was as strong as ever and our marriage was going to be one of those testimonial stories of forgiveness and restoration, and he would come out the other side a kind, loving man with the perfect ending. Is that what happened in my situation? No, but God has still made the impossible possible in so many other impossible situations on this journey.

The free will that God gave us includes our choice to choose love, but that choice also comes with freedom to make the very opposite choice. God will never make anyone love Him, nor will He interfere with the bad choice you're making. The plan may not be working out as planned or purposed *but* don't fret. God knows. He sees, He cares, He loves, and He loves *you.*

I think about it this way. Every choice you make, whether small or big, has an effect, a ripple that goes out into the sphere of your influence. It ripples into the layers that you have effect on, and you may not even see or know in your life time how far your ripple effect goes, but trust me: it goes and goes and goes.

It could be a good effect you're having on those around you, or it could be bad, but every choice you make has its ripples.

As the effect of your choices ripple into eternity, you need to always be aware that they're effects from the very choices you're making right now today. Always think bigger and outside of your own little bubble when making big decisions: that would be my advice if you were asking for any, and if you weren't looking for any, it's pretty good advice, so you can take it anyway.

I made a big decision to stay in a marriage and choose to continue to love and make changes in myself. It may not have been the right choice to the very end, but it helped me grow and stay in line with the Word of God and His plan for my life.

Now as I look back, I know that staying in an emotionally (or any type of) abusive relationship is not ever the right thing to do. If you're reading this and currently in an abusive relationship, physically or emotionally, please seek help and talk to someone you trust to get you help. Your health and safety is more important than your reputation.

I chose to get help from a professional counselor, all the while being told by my now estranged husband that he couldn't stand me or being near me. He chose no help, no ownership of his actions or words, and at times he pretended things hadn't even happened or been said. I made a choice to get help and not run to try to find something to instantly satisfy my immediate desires or feelings to "feel good," using people or drugs or shopping or food that, long term, would hurt me.

I have repeated this a few times over the pages because if I had someone point out to me other than my family that certain things were not normal and I should seek help, I think I'd have looked for help a lot earlier on. This got real and deep quickly, so I probably need to remind you that the person I tell you about was someone who over two years had made choice after choice to not only run from God but was choosing death over life. There was a lot spiritually going on for him, and that possibly is why he couldn't stand being around me, because he couldn't stand Christ that was in me. Don't forget who the real enemy is, no matter what circumstance you're going through or who it is. Satan will use anyone and anything he can; never underestimate the schemes of the real Enemy.

The longer I stayed to love my estranged husband, the worse it got. The deeper I dug into Jesus, the more my husband at the time seemed to be full of hate and rage toward me. I'd utter the word *Jesus* under my breath in fear, and the look I'd get from the other side of the room is not even explainable.

If he ever heard me from afar praying, it would throw him into a state of confusion, and at times, he would demand to know what I was saying. His behavior did start to intimidate me, and that's when I realized he wasn't even the man I knew anymore, and the kind of love I was giving him wasn't the kind of love he needed.

He needed tough love that exposed the darkness and evil in his ways and words, but I didn't know how to give that kind of love. I had heard about it and some people close to me who could see things that I couldn't at the time also suggested this "tough love."

Shortly after realizing it was tough love that was needed, people in my world who knew what was happening in my life at the time saw things I couldn't see with my own eyes. Almost every other male friend or family in my life at the time, whether it be my dad, brother-in-law, friends, work colleagues, all said the same phrase over and over to me, as if they had all gotten the same memo that I missed. They didn't even necessarily know each other, so it wasn't as if they'd all met and talked about the best option for me. The phrase "you need to get yourself a lawyer" was the same phrase they all had said in conversations with me within a few days of seeing them all separately.

If I'm going to be completely honest, it scared me so much I was willing to just give up on the whole situation, pack my bags, and get on the next plane to a land far, far away. I was full of shame at this time. I wasn't brave enough to share some of what was going on in my life, but it's not a topic to be tiptoed around or ignored.

It's real, and there are too many woman and men out there feeling alone, full of shame and bound with no way out. But there is a way through and out, and the good news in any situation is that God is with us! *Immanuel* means "God with us." That means even when you don't feel like He is, even when you can't hear His voice or His word doesn't seem to be talking to you, or you literally feel so alone it's like you're in a submarine at the bottom of the Pacific Ocean alone in a dark cave with nothing even around you, not even a giant octopus—God is still there!

I've been there. Trust me: I know exactly how you're feeling or have felt if you've felt like that before. For a good six months, my estranged husband tried to convince me Jesus wasn't real, God was a fake, all our friends were fake, and everyone at our church was fake. I'd sit there thinking, *This is so ridiculous. How did we even get here to this point of conversation? You can't tell me God, whom I have experienced personally, is not real.*

To get this into perspective, you can't sit me in a red room with red floors and walls, red furniture, and a glowing red light and then tell me until the cows come home that it's a blue room with blue walls and floors and furniture and that I'm seeing and experiencing everything wrong. It sounds insane, does it not? Insane is almost how I felt in that moment, sitting there trying to figure out how to respond without making him angry. It was then that I think I realized there was way more going on than I realized.

My husband at the time wasn't the real enemy either, and I had to constantly remind myself to not get distracted and let my heart get hard and bitter. Did I just say that? Yes, I did. It doesn't matter who it was or what they did to you. If you can get that revelation that they aren't your real enemy, you'll get the upper hand and start to see the real Enemy and all his schemes, plans, and tricks he is trying to throw your way. You'll see them coming before the Enemy even gets a chance to get a foot in the door of your situation or circumstance, and you can be a step in front every time!

I've read the book people! and in the end of the book, Jesus conquers death and wins, which ultimately means you and I have the victory. We may lose some battles on the way, but we have won the war. We are the head and not the tail.

> The LORD will make you the head, not the tail. If you pay attention to the commands of the LORD your God that I give you this day and carefully follow them, you will always be at the top, never at the bottom. Deuteronomy 28:13

You and I have the same power of Christ in us, and He is enough. That's the same power that raised Christ from the grave! Do you read this and actually believe it with all your heart, soul, and mind? I'm giving you permission (not that you need it), but if you need a little nudge toward dream bigger, think bigger—God is bigger! If you're a believer, then *you* are enough because Christ *is* in you!

> I also pray that you will understand the incredible greatness of God's power for us who believe him. This is the same mighty power that raised Christ from the dead and seated him in the place of honor at God's right hand in the heavenly realms. Ephesians 1:19–20

Do you actually believe that today in your situation?
If you don't, it's not enough for me to try and pump you up

about it, but I really encourage you to get alone and search the Word
for all the scriptures you can possibly find on your circumstance.
The Word of God covers everything in life we could possibly face.
It's the only guide you'll ever need in life, let's be honest.

All this sidetrack is to say that my estranged spouse's choices
rippled into and over my life and had many disastrous effects. But
God is actually bigger than our choices, so although someone in your
life may be making decisions that lead to death not life, affecting
you directly to cause hurt, pain, and dysfunction, God has still got
this! He still goes before you and makes a way.

Be encouraged today by this: God can use the very thing that
is trying to destroy you to restore you! You will never come second
for putting God first in your life and your children's lives. There's
no choice anyone else can make that can stop God's blessing and
favor in your future, it's only your own choices that can run you
into darkness.

God will still have His perfect will and way in your life. And
that's where my friend, He shows up and turns the impossible into
possible. God's word never fails and never returns void.

> So is my word that goes out from my mouth: it will
> not return to me empty, but will accomplish what
> I desire and achieve the purpose for which I sent it.
> Isaiah 55:11

I remember almost every word said to me, which felt like knives
cutting through my heart—the feeling of confusion and emptiness
the night my then husband told me he no longer wanted to be
around me, couldn't stand to be around me, didn't love me anymore.
And then he wouldn't give me any explanation as to why.

He was the person I trusted fully and gave my all to. He was the
one that I had his back no matter what. I was his biggest cheerleader.
He was the only one I had eyes for, and I was completely devoted
to him. But just like that I felt like the earth was ripped out from

underneath me, and as I fell into this big, black abyss, my world spun out of control. It didn't even feel like a reality.

He traveled a lot for work, and in the month leading up to that night he left, he had become distant. Day after day, it got to the point that he was working from seven a.m. till eight or nine p.m., but my trust in him was so much that if he said he was working, I just believed him. I would never have thought he'd have an affair.

Part of being in an emotionally abusive relationship can make you question yourself every time and make you feel like you're alone and on your own. If I'd ever have confronted him or asked him if he was having an affair, I'd have been yelled at to not be so stupid, or I'd have been called a psycho, which would lead to an argument, and then I'd be told it was all my fault.

There was unusual behavior by him and suspicion from me since we were teenagers that he may have not been devoted to me, although I was always shut right down at any attempt to have the conversation. But the repeated words thrown on you by someone you love and trusted for over half your life taints the way you think and creates strongholds you actually cannot just break away from so easily.

I share this with you only because I hope that if you're reading this and feel deep inside your spirit that you know and believe what God says about you and know the difference now between truth and lie but can't seem to shake of the lies still, you would get some professional help from a psychologist who has dealt with emotional abuse as well as reminding yourself daily and washing your mind with exactly God thinks and says of you.

> Because of the Lord's great love we are not consumed, for his compassions never fail. They are new every morning; great is your faithfulness. Lamentations 3:22–23

But he said to me, "My grace is sufficient for you, for my power is made perfect in weakness. "Therefore I will boast all the more gladly about my weaknesses, so that Christ's power may rest on me. 2 Corinthians 12:9

Your eyes saw my unformed body; all the days ordained for me were written in your book before one of them came to be. Psalm 139:16

And we know that in all things God works for the good of those who love him, who have been called according to his purpose. Romans 8:28

For I know the plans I have for you," declares the Lord, "plans to prosper you and not to harm you, plans to give you hope and a future. Jeremiah 29:11

Read that again and read it out loud,

I have a distinct memory of a night when I was dating my estranged husband, I was about seventeen years old. It was a repeat of nasty words thrown around, bad behavior, his normal outlet of punching holes in walls and throwing things at me, which turned into regrettable things being said to each other. At this time in my life, this wasn't at all the normal things I had experienced in my own family or childhood, but it had become normal in my relationship with him.

I can't remember what the actual argument was about, nor can I remember what was said word for word, but neither of us back then knew the love of God, and we weren't in a relationship with Jesus, so the words said were most definitely regrettable.

I share that with you because that night I felt as though I had nowhere to go, and no one to talk to about what was going on. Sometimes you let things become normal because no one has told you it isn't supposed to be that way, but I'm telling you it isn't supposed to be that way. In these moments, it felt as if the windows were closing and the room was getting darker. I didn't understand what the feeling was then, but my spirit always sensed something wrong.

My thoughts went into chaos, and my mind believed the lies. It was as if I was inside a room full of shame, alone and away from my friends and family. I'd always find a way to justify bad behavior and feel sorry for him. I remember the tears and anger in his eyes as he shared things from his past and childhood, things that were not fair, things that were out of his control, as he was a child.

That was always what drove the justification in my mind that his behavior was OK because he didn't know any better and he would have no problem pouring out his heart to how poor his childhood was. That fact is very much true—he had a rubbish childhood and experiences, but it doesn't make it right to stay in that dysfunctional circle.

As children, we learn everything we know about relationships and life in general from those around us. So if we do not have a stable consistent role model as we are growing and learning then whatever we see modelled is what our normal will be, even if it's not healthy.

Although I wasn't yet married to him at this stage of my life, that night I felt like there was no escape from the relationship. I loved him and was devoted to only him, but my immaturity and shame kept me feeling trapped and alone in the situation I found myself in almost daily. That night, as I sat on the cold tile floor of an old dusty sunroom, I felt like it was the beginning of the end because I believed the lies of the enemy, not just in that moment that night but for over a year already, whispers that I simply wasn't enough.

I had a loving family around me but not as many friends of my own anymore. I could have reached out and asked someone for advice but for some reason, whether it was the shame or immaturity, I just didn't know what to do with the feelings of being lost, alone and trapped. One thing I know now that I didn't know then was that even though I may have felt alone, I most definitely was not.

> Be strong and courageous. Do not be afraid or terrified because of them, for the Lord your God goes with you; he will never leave you nor forsake you. Deuteronomy 31:6

There are people around who loved and cared for me, but more importantly I had a Father in heaven who not only loved and cared for me but with no judgement whatsoever. He also wants and knows what's best for me even when I don't understand what is best for me.

I know you may already know all of this, but I need to remind myself on a daily basis. The whirlwinds of everyday life get me distracted, and if I'm not constantly reminding myself and renewing my mind with God's word, then I fall into the trap of my own thoughts, discouragement, and doubt.

I think I could look back on the past fourteen years and think, *What a waste! Or why couldn't I see it when it was plain and simple?* I can pinpoint almost every bad choice and cover up that my estranged partner made, which I then covered with an excuse or justification.

Or maybe I can look back and blame myself, even feel sorry for myself, and get stuck in a battlefield in my own mind.

It's just so easy to get caught up in distraction after distraction and, before you know it, run down the path of doubt and shame that keeps you stuck and doesn't allow you to grow, learn, and love as God has planned for you.

I'm saying it to you, but I'm actually speaking about myself. I've been there, I've done that, and by the grace of God, He picked me up every time and gave me a million second chances.

Praise God there's a second option, and I can choose to see a God Almighty that keeps His promises over my life, who goes before and behind me, who protects and covers me with His love that endures forever.

I can choose to learn from the past and move forward into my destiny and calling and so can *you*!

chapter 6

God's Love Is Enough

Am I Even Enough?

I often wondered if I was the only one who's ever asked themselves that question. But where I've come to in my own life, I have a strong feeling I'm not the only one out there who asks the question—possibly even daily.

Every time I ask myself if I'm enough, I feel like Jack and Jill falling down the hill of self-doubt and self-pity. It was like the pump factor would get me sprinting and stomping up the trail, thinking, *I'm good enough.* I didn't need to hold the rope or rails as the climb got steeper—I'd just pump myself up:

Get it, girl! You know who you are, where you're going, and what you're doing! Just press in harder, girl! Don't stop—you're not a quitter! I was made for this! Now watch me get it!

It's all fun and games until fear creeps in or someone says something to trigger doubt and negativity. Then your pump factor deflates almost immediately, and it all sounds a bit more like this:

I can't do it. I'm so not qualified to even think about this let alone do it. If I get myself in too deep, I won't be able to get out, and it's going to be embarrassing. It's just too overwhelming to even think about; it's just not meant to be. Everyone is going to see me fail and fall flat on my face, so I just can't do this.

And that's the moment the big red button of fear and doubt is pressed, and I'd slip and fall down the hill of self-pity, doubt, and shame. I've learned the pump factor can be great for some moments in your life, but if you have nothing to hold onto when you slip (which is God's truth about you and His word), you'll fall back down the hill.

It took me over ten years of following Jesus to get this revelation. You may already have, but if you don't, get this is your spirit:

If you're building yourself up with yourself, who are you going to grab hold of when your foot slips on fear or doubt? When you're climbing on the self-pump factor, you haven't prepared safety nets, ropes, or rails for your climb.

It's all you, baby, and you feel ready to conquer the world on your pump factor, but before you conquer the world, you need to let God conquer the castle you've built inside that you're standing on to cheer yourself on.

Let God rebuild from the very foundations. What He'll build is far beyond anything you could have ever built on your own, and better yet, you won't be needing to knock it down and rebuild it later on in life because God sets the right foundations for exactly what you need in the future as well.

He'll add the extensions needed at the perfect timing and can do so because the foundation is set right and can handle any extra architect needed in your future.

The Two Foundations

So everyone who hears these words of Mine and acts on them, will be like a wise man [a far-sighted, practical, and sensible man] who built his house on the rock. And the rain fell, and the floods and torrents came, and the winds blew and slammed against that house; yet it did not fall, because it had been founded on the rock. And everyone who hears these words of Mine and does not do them, will be like a foolish (stupid) man who built his house on the sand. And the rain fell, and the floods and torrents came, and the winds blew and slammed against that house; and it fell—and great and complete was its fall. Matthew 7:24–27

Have it written on your heart that God is with you always, God is your strength, God is your protector, God is your refuge and safe hiding place, God will provide all you need, and God will build you up. You don't need to try and build yourself. You just need to arm and guard yourself with His word and truth so you can grab hold when you feel your foot starting to slip.

If you build your inner castle on God's word, then when the rain of doubt falls, the winds of shame slam against you, the floods of negativity and loneliness try to push you down, you won't fall down because you're built on the strong foundation of God's word, and He will uphold you.

I will build you up again, and you Virgin Israel, will be rebuilt. Again you will take up your timbrels and go out to dance with joyful. Jeremiah 31:4

If you let God build you up, no one can tear you down. Let your foundations be built up from God's word and revelation; then no trip or slip will send you tumbling down the hillside of self-doubt and pity because you'll have His promises and word as your safety net, rope, and rail to hold tightly onto as you get back up to stand on your feet.

I cannot encourage you enough to always go back to the Word of God. His words never return void which means He turns up, maybe not how you expect or think He will, but He doesn't fail,

He doesn't falter, and His promise over your life will never fail or return to you empty.

Some of you might be reading this and thinking, *Great, I hear what you're saying, and I believe it, but there's just one problem, and it's not my belief. But it's just not that easy for me to trust. What if I confess it out loud and nothing changes when I wake up tomorrow?*

Here is the deal. You probably will wake up tomorrow and still be in the same situation, circumstance, pain, or problem, *but* God doesn't do surface-level works on the outside. God looks at the heart and works the only way to make a real, lasting change: from the inside out. And the longer you're in the situation or circumstance, the closer you are to God's plan of breakthrough, so let Him work, and while He works, your job is to confess and tell your soul daily that His promises never fail.

> Cast your burden on the Lord [release it] and He will sustain and uphold you; He will never allow the righteous to be shaken (slip, fall, fail). Psalm 55:22

> If you stay in this land, I will build you up and not tear you down; I will plant you and not uproot you, for I have relented concerning the disaster I have inflicted on you. Jeremiah 42:10

> Don't be afraid, for I am with you. Don't be discouraged, for I am your God. I will strengthen you and help you. I will hold you up with my victorious right hand. Isaiah 41:10

> For I hold you by your right hand— I, the Lord your God. And I say to you, Don't be afraid. I am here to help you. Isaiah 41:13

I keep my eyes always on the Lord. With him at my right hand, I will not be shaken. Psalm 16:8

The Lord is my rock, my fortress and my deliverer; my God is my rock, in whom I take refuge, my shield and the horn of my salvation, my stronghold. Psalm 18:2

The Lord is my light and my salvation so why should I be afraid? The Lord is my fortress, protecting me from danger, so why should I tremble? Psalm 27:1

He only is my rock and my salvation, my fortress; I shall not be shaken. Psalm 62:6

Being confident of this, that he who began a good work in you will carry it on to completion until the day of Christ Jesus. Philippians 1:6

And my God will meet all your needs according to the riches of his glory in Christ Jesus. Philippians 4:19

So do not throw away your confidence; it will be richly rewarded. You need to persevere so that when you have done the will of God, you will receive what he has promised. Hebrews 10:35–36

God is our refuge and strength mighty and impenetrable, A very present and well-proved help in trouble. Therefore we will not fear, though the earth should change And though the mountains be shaken and slip into the heart of the seas, Though its waters roar and foam, Though the mountains tremble at its roaring. Selah.

Psalm 46:1–3

Any troubled thoughts I had about myself I'd tell myself I'm the only one that thinks these thoughts, but one thing I've learned on this journey of rising above the betrayal, lies, shame, and emotional abuse is that the Enemy will do his best to try and keep you in isolation with your own thoughts.

Let's get real here. In case no one has ever told you before, stop thinking those thoughts right now! Catch them, label them with lie, and throw them right out.

After over eleven years of following Jesus and knowing deep down in my heart what God thinks and says about me, I still have to choose daily what trail I let my thoughts go down. And, yes, my struggle is real almost every day. I need to make sure daily that I'm catching the thoughts that don't align with what the Word of God says about me.

> Yet in all these things we are more than conquerors and gain an overwhelming victory through Him who loved us [so much that He died for us]. For I am convinced [and continue to be convinced— beyond any doubt] that neither death, nor life, nor angels, nor principalities, nor things present and threatening, nor things to come, nor powers, nor height, nor depth, nor any other created thing, will be able to separate us from the [unlimited] love of God, which is in Christ Jesus our Lord. Romans 8:37–39

chapter 7

Don't Settle on Distractions

In the midst of all that's going on, even before trouble comes, I already know how it's going to end, and it ends in victory.

The Enemy wants us stuck and scared, unable to face battles because we're afraid that we will lose, but God has told us we'll face struggles. He also says He'll never leave us and that we are the head and not the tail.

So believe God and His word today. Find the promises in His word and read them out loud over and over again until you believe in the very bottom of your soul.

My journey hasn't come to an end, so I know that there'll be more struggles to face in the days and years to come, but more so, I know that we're more than conquerors. We've already gained an overwhelming victory through Jesus in the things to come.

Know that whatever you're going through, you're not staying there. You'll pass through it, you'll come out the other end, and most importantly, you'll know that Jesus is with you. Why is it happening to you? I don't know. I don't even know, nor will I ever have to know, why the darkest things that I've experienced have happened. But I know that when I passed through and came out the other side, I was stronger, wiser, and closer to God than ever before.

God is always as close as you let Him be. It's not Him getting closer to us. It's us allowing ourselves and our hearts to come closer to His.

If you're sitting at the bottom of the valley right now in your situation or circumstance and you're scared to get up and start the climb up your mountain, I want to tell you, sweet one, you're not alone. Be assured that God is with you.

The road looks rocky and unsafe but He has made a way. This is where your faith kicks in. You can't see, so you must have faith that He has gone before you in the unseen.

We aren't handed faith on a platter. It's a choice. We choose to have faith. There is no magic mountain that faith physically falls from where we can go and catch it. I've sat at the foot of my mountain with tears falling down my face, petrified of what it would mean for me to climb the unknown peak that was in front of me. I can't remember even experiencing anxiety until this last season in my life. I was so crippled with fear I couldn't even take the first step because I didn't know how.

I was clinging to a dangerous, destructive, broken, wobbly bridge that was trying to shake me off into the pit of death below, and all because of the fear that was driving me I had chosen to hold fast to that destructive, deadly bridge for years instead of choosing to start the climb.

I know what it's like for fear to be so thick it turns into a cloud that slowly descends like a roof over your head and you can no longer see what life should look like at the peak of the mountain as you stand at the foot of it.

You know there's more inside of you that burns to accomplish what God has for your life, but you just don't know how because the descending clouds are so thick and heavy that they've formed a roof that's holding you down.

If I could attempt to explain in words what the years leading up to the moment of me taking the first step out in faith to climb my mountain looked like—this would be as close as I could get. But remember: there's no fear in God's love. Choosing to believe His perfect love drives out fear, and so I stepped out, trusting. Although I couldn't physically or spiritually see how or where my foot would step, I knew in my innermost being that God loved me so much and that His word promises He will not leave or forsake us or even let our foot slip.

He'll not let your foot slip—he who watches over you will not slumber. Psalm 121:3

I was at a summer camp/retreat, and funny enough, the preacher's sermon was actually on climbing your mountain.

At the end of the night he called people down the front for prayer, and before I could even look up, my feet were already racing me down to the front. This was even a surprise to me that I'd just go down by myself to the front, in a place that I had only been to for the first time and knew only a handful of people who were back up at the seats where I was sitting.

So there I found myself, tears flooding down my face as I decided to take the first step. I still had no idea what that step was, but I knew in my heart that if God was going to direct me, then no matter how hard it was, I was committed to taking the first step. And I would follow wherever He led me.

As I stood there in a puddle of my own tears, I looked up and couldn't even see because my eyes were so full of flowing tears. So I just stood there feeling completely out of my comfort zone with my head hung down, and in that split-second moment of thinking *Maybe I should just abandon ship and run to the bathroom and hang out in there until I can stop this river of tears*, one of the retreat leaders in the front row whose voice wasn't familiar to me came and put her hands on my shoulders and began to pray.

She began to pray instantly and gently. She started to pray for God's strength over me and then began to repeat the word *courage*. I still remember the sound of her voice as she said to me, "I feel like the one thing God really wants to say to you is take courage." She would go on again and continue to pray but would stop again and say, "Courage, courage, courage." If I'd have counted the number of times I heard, "Take courage," without exaggerating I think it would have been at least fifty times, and it was strong in my spirit to receive it.

That night, I went back to the hotel, and as I was faced with my mountain, I almost forgot the words spoken over me. It wasn't until the next day, driving back home to Sydney with my estranged husband in silence in a hostile car, I was left to my own thoughts, and I pondered the last twenty-four hours and all that God had spoken to me about.

I opened the notes on my phone, and as I started to read, I remembered that in the book of Joshua, it's repeated over and again to be strong and courageous. So I looked it up, desperate to find out how I could be more courageous. I kept thinking, *How in the world can I be any more courageous, God? What in the world have I been doing the last twelve months, hanging on for dear life to you, your word, and your promises? Is that not courageous enough?*

> No one will be able to stand against you all the days of your life. As I was with Moses, so I will be with you; I will never leave you nor forsake you. Be strong and courageous, because you will lead these people to inherit the land I swore to their ancestors to give them.
> "Be strong and very courageous. Be careful to obey all the law my servant Moses gave you; do not turn from it to the right or to the left, that you may be successful wherever you go. Keep this Book of the Law always on your lips; meditate on it day and night, so that you may be careful to do everything written in it. Then you will be prosperous and successful. Have I not commanded

you? Be strong and courageous. Do not be afraid;
do not be discouraged, for the Lord your God will
be with you wherever you go." Joshua 1:5–9

Here is what I learned that week: courage is not a pill you can
take once and wash down with a shot of something strong, and then
bing bang boom, you are off on this journey in life full of strength
and courage—no, no, no.

It's a daily dose you must choose to take from our God Almighty.
God will give you strength. You don't need to beg or search for it,
for when we are weak, He *is* strong,

So I am well pleased with weakness, with insults,
with distresses, with persecutions, and with
difficulties, for the sake of Christ; for when I am
weak, then I am strong. 2 Corinthians 12:10

We have this opportunity, no matter how difficult life gets or
what the days are throwing our way, to take strength and courage
from our Father in heaven who comes down right into our very heart
and soul to give us the strength and courage to live each day to the
fullest in His plan and purpose for our lives.

I looked up the word *courage* in three different English
dictionaries:

Merriam-Webster's Collegiate Dictionary: "mental or moral
strength to venture, persevere, and withstand danger, fear or
difficulty"

Oxford Living Dictionaries: "the ability to do something that
frightens one; bravery"

Cambridge Dictionary: "the ability to control your fear in a
dangerous or difficult situation."

I found it interesting that the definitions each covered the very things I needed the courage for as I journeyed through the darkest days of my life. God is so kind that He met me and continues to meet me where I'm to give me the strength and courage I need for everything I have faced in my past and will face in the future.

I'm beyond confident that God will never fail me, and I want to tell you that He'll not fail *you* either, He loves you, and He knows exactly how He is going to work the very thing you think is going to take you out and turn it right around for your good and His glory. I want to remind you right now in this moment that nothing is too hard for Him. No mountain is too big—God is bigger.

I know I've echoed it throughout the pages you've already read, but I just want to say it again: God is kind and loves me and you so much that I really feel the need to say again that if you somehow have any other feelings or images of God and His character that don't reflect kindness and love, then ask Him to shine His light on whatever it is that is tainting it and let God reveal His true character to you.

He's a God who wants what's best for us.

> For I know the plans I have for you, declares the Lord, plans for welfare and not for evil, to give you a future and a hope. His love for us is beyond measure. Jeremiah 29:11

> But God shows his love for us in that while we were still sinners, Christ died for us. God is love and there is no greater love any one can have for us than the love God has for us. Romans 5:8

> In this is love, not that we have loved God but that he loved us and sent his Son to be the propitiation for our sins. He is a good Father who sacrificed for us when we did not know any better. 1 John 4:10

For God so loved the world, that he gave his only Son, that whoever believes in him should not perish but have eternal life. He is a God who gives us what we need, He is our peace and our strength. John 3:16

Have you not known? Have you not heard? The Lord is the everlasting God, the Creator of the ends of the earth. He does not faint or grow weary; his understanding is unsearchable. He gives power to the faint, and to him who has no might he increases strength. Even youths shall faint and be weary, and young men shall fall exhausted; but they who wait for the Lord shall renew their strength; they shall mount up with wings like eagles; they shall run and not be weary; they shall walk and not faint. Isaiah 40:28–31

He's a good Father who cares for you, all the way down to the smallest detail, and will uphold you.

Fear not, for I am with you; be not dismayed, for I am your God; I will strengthen you, I will help you, I will uphold you with my righteous right hand. Isaiah 41:10

He Is a God who will protect you like no other.

This God—his way is perfect; the word of the Lord proves true; he is a shield for all those who take refuge in him. He is a fair and just Father, Psalm 18:30

God is fair and just; He corrects the misdirected,
Sends them in the right direction.

He gives the rejects his hand, And leads them
step-by-step. From now on every road you travel
Will take you to God. Follow the Covenant signs;
Read the charted directions Psalm 25:8–10

chapter 8

Keep Your Focus on Jesus
(No Matter How Big the Storm
Blows around You)

If you've been on the journey with Jesus as your main man for a while, you've possibly had the moments where you get away with Him alone so you can pray and pour your heart out knowing that if you wait and linger, you'll hear the small, still, soft voice raise hope within you.

Sometimes I can use the most dramatic voice filled with hundreds of words, or be a blubbering mess with no words and just tears flowing, or maybe even just a "God, SOS, i need help. I don't know what to say let alone pray."

But every time I take the time to get away with Him, whether it's sitting cliffside with nothing but ocean in front of me, or sitting in the car alone because I've arrived at the next destination a little early, or (let's be honest—way less glamorous than oceanfront) sitting on restroom floor with the door locked because the kids are busy doing something and finally, for once, have let me go to the bathroom alone, the Holy Spirit will whisper into my heart and bring scripture to mind.

No matter how many words I use, the funny thing is that every time God gives me the shortest but sweetest promise in reply. I've learned that sometimes God will give you revelations and promises that you can share with others, but sometimes He'll give you words to hold onto and not share with anyone, something just for you to spur you onward and upward with hope, to let you know that He cares about the smallest of details.

On a side note, in my walk with Jesus, I learned probably way later than most people the importance of not just reading my Bible daily but memorizing key scriptures so that when the time comes and you need to pull from what is within you, the Word of God is what will come out.

It's not rocket science, but if the Word is not in there, it won't come out.

That's not to say God can't or won't use other ways of getting a word or an encouragement to you, but He has given us the greatest guide and weapon we'll ever need, which we can use at all times, and that is His word (the sword of the spirit).

The most special moments I've encountered with my heavenly Father, I haven't shared with anyone because even if I did, they wouldn't understand just how special it was and what it meant, and that's OK.

As much as I want to shout from the rooftop on a daily basis how good, kind, and loving God is to me, some moments were just meant for me, and the same will be for you. They are moments to cherish and tuck away deep into your heart, not to leave buried but to treasure and have as reminders when you need them most.

I've learned over the last few years that God is so personal that down to the very smallest details of your life does He care. If you take time in your days and weeks to stop worrying about all the things that aren't going right, you might just see in the smallest of details that wouldn't mean anything to anyone else apart from you, that God is working beauty from your ashes.

As I type this, I feel so heavy in my heart to spur those who find themselves reading these simple words on these simple pages that God cares so personally about you and your needs. In fact, He knows more than you do the very things you need, and just like the good Father He is, He won't hold back from you. It just may not look like what you think you need or want right now.

I don't share this story lightly because I don't want it interpreted any other way than how God showed me—He knows what is best for me. I'll take you right back to a few years ago in early 2015. Although with God by my side I knew that I'd never be alone, I actually didn't understand that to the fullest until now two years later.

I was completely overcome with fear about what it meant for me to be a single mom. I was completely full of fear because I didn't know how the kids could grow up without a father no matter how unhealthy and toxic the relationship was. I thought that if the front was up, then I could make it work behind the scenes, and it made me desperate to hang on to the very thing that was poisoning me and my children.

Because from my own experience I had only ever seen bad come out of a divorce. The mess, the dysfunction, and the poor children in the middle that always ended up shattered and broken was the only experience I had witnessed.

On top of everything else, I've learned along the way. I have a new revelation that almost everything we fear is because we don't know.

We fear what we don't know because we don't understand, and we don't understand because we don't know, so it's a little bit like a tragic circle we can get ourselves into about anything if we aren't careful to take a step back and look at things from a different angle while asking God to give us eyes to see and ears to hear what He has for us in the situations we find ourselves full of fear in.

Sorry I got sidetracked, but back to it.

After almost two months of early mornings, late nights and working weekends nonstop were a buildup of longer hours away since I had babies. I was under this delusion of this man I had defended since the day I'd met him as a young teenage girl that because I felt sorry for him and his past and loved him, he'd never leave me. I was committed, till death us do part, even though I cried myself to sleep many nights, feeling stuck and alone. I was the one who stuck by everything he had done and said, all the drama, all the hate and negativity, all the spiritual ugly that I just thought was his normal and wouldn't change, all the emotional abuse over half my life, it all brought me to this one point about two years ago.

It was almost midnight, and I found myself on my knees in front of this man who I think is my husband, but I'm actually not sure because I'm numb from head to toe. I'm in so much confusion I actually don't feel like I'm even really on earth. I don't know how else to explain the feeling.

There I was, begging for an answer why as I knelt in front of him, sitting on the lounge with his face turned away from me as he couldn't even look at me.

I was in a delusion that nothing was wrong and there was no buildup. In this moment, I couldn't see the buildup over the last few years, a delusion all of a sudden that there had to be something wrong with me and if whatever was happening right then was ending in me being alone and left out for what felt like secondhand trash, then I couldn't even comprehend what the next minute looked like and how to even breathe in.

I had no idea at the time, but I was in a full-blown panic attack. If this all sounds a little dramatic to you, that's because it was. The words of what I felt and thought in that split second of him mumbling, "It's not going to work anymore," with no explanation of even what's not going to work anymore, knocked not just the wind out of me but almost the life.

Kneeling there on the floor was like an out-of-body experience, and I think after I cried all the tears that were physically able to come out, I walked to bed and went to sleep. I remember waking up that morning, thinking, *Was this all a dream last night? Did that really even happen?*

But as I turned around, just like every morning the last few months, he wasn't there. He was already up and ready to walk out the door to work. That's when the weight of the night before fell hard back down and hit me, almost knocking the very breath out of me.

I had no idea what to do or what to say. The only thing that came to mind was *Why do you have to be at work at seven in the morning when you used to have to only be there at nine? Why do you get home at eight or nine at night? I can never contact you beforehand and you never eat dinner when you get home.*

But the words would never come. Every time I thought it, maybe because I knew deep down inside he was living a lie, hiding from me way more than he hides from the rest of the world that I had covered up for him because I thought I was protecting him.

You see, in the past if I'd asked these questions in a joking voice, "Are you a double agent or really working as a spy?" I was ignored, and if I followed it with, "Are you having an affair?" I was shut right down with how stupid and paranoid I was. If I responded again, I was shut down harder with how controlling I was with him.

Every so often, it was thrown in randomly that I didn't let him have his own friends and other randomly timed hurtful things directed to or about me. It would always make me feel suspicious, but ultimately, it made me feel like it was a stupid question and my fault for even asking.

Did any of this make sense to me? Absolutely not. If anything, it all felt the total opposite, but I felt stuck and at times a little crazy in my own thoughts. The reason I share some very specific parts is because if you're reading this and you realize your environment is the same or something is hitting a sore spot for you, then I want to encourage you to talk to someone safe about your situation. If you don't have anyone in your life you can trust, then call your local domestic violence shelter, which will be able to talk things out with you.

I didn't speak to someone earlier because I thought that if I did, they would think there was something wrong with me or judge me. And if they didn't judge me, then they probably wouldn't even believe me, so there was no point.

I was so low in my self-esteem from the years of emotional abuse that I couldn't get past the picket fence in my head that was holding me back from getting help. I call it a picket fence because it was just that, a small, frail barrier that I could have stepped over and out of, but I didn't have the strength or knowledge of how to.

I had to choose not to go and throw my own pity party, and continue to make that choice, monthly at times, as low blows were thrown that I knew were far from the truth. I had to surround myself with ones I trusted and have the truth from God's word engraved on my heart so that when the Enemy whispered lies (and he will—don't underestimate how low and evil the Enemy will go to try and steal your joy), but I'm writing to the one who reads and understands what I mean.

If you have never been through an experience like this (because not everyone has or will), you'll never actually understand fully, and that's that OK. Not everyone understood the choices I started to make, even when they were choices made with a pure heart and a word from God.

My own family could see over the years all the alarming behavior, and yet I still defended him and blamed his past for his current behavior. I was stuck in the belief that he wouldn't change even though he had been given chance after chance, so I just needed to deal with it.

Let me pause there for a second and say something I want you to read and let sink in: that is a lie and far from the truth, God never planned and purposed for you to be in a relationship that's harmful. God created relationship. He created us to be in a beautiful relationship with Himself and other people.

Love God first and foremost and then love each other is our

greatest commandment, and I believe we are to love each other equally not rule over each other or harm one another.

> Love the Lord your God with all your heart and with all your soul and with all your mind and with all your strength. Mark 12:30

Could it be that our relationships with one another have the power to reflect the very character of God to those around us?

> Love is patient and kind; love does not envy or boast; it is not arrogant or rude. It does not insist on its own way; it is not irritable or resentful; it does not rejoice at wrongdoing, but rejoices with the truth. Love bears all things, believes all things, hopes all things, endures all things. 1 Corinthians 13:4–7

This scripture is the prime example of love, and God is love, so if we are truly living this verse out, then we are reflecting the very love of God.

I was convinced that I could "love" my estranged husband back to God. I started asking God to change me, mold me, shape me, work in me, Lord, with all you have to increase my patience, help me be kinder, open my eyes not to envy others or boast in myself. I'd get on my knees daily to ask God to create in me a clean heart that held no resentment and clung to the truth only.

> Repay no one evil for evil, but give thought to do what is honorable in the sight of all.
>
> If possible, so far as it depends on you, live peaceably with all. Beloved, never avenge yourselves, but leave it to the wrath of God, for it is written, "Vengeance is mine, I will repay, says the Lord." To

> the contrary, "if your enemy is hungry, feed him;
> if he is thirsty, give him something to drink; for by
> so doing you will heap burning coals on his head."
> Do not be overcome by evil, but overcome evil with
> good. Romans 12:17–21

That's all good, sweet, and all things lovely to ask God for, but don't ask Him if you're not ready for Him to actually do the good works in you. I'm going to keep it real with you—it's not easy. I'm not going to sugarcoat the reality of what comes with God doing a good work in your life, but that's exactly what it is—it's a good work, and the pain is worth it.

I have this new saying that's not that profound, but it was a slap in the right direction every time I doubted. It's as simple as "no pain, no gain." I was right in trying to love this man I once knew but the love I was giving was coming from a blinded, hurting girl. It wasn't the tough love he actually needed. I was giving him permission to continue down the path of bitterness, hate, jealousy, recklessness, slander, abusive, selfishness.

I needed to let him go and let God.

At the time, I thought it was going to be this perfect fairytale ending of him finding his way back to God, and all my pain and hurt would just disappear, and we'd live happily ever after, pointing others toward God's love and building the church together. I trusted God wholeheartedly, but I thought my plan was good enough to be His.

I often put God in a box, and just when I think I've finally not put Him a box, I take a step back and see I've actually done it again, but this time it's just a bigger box. My plan wasn't God's plan, but God's plan was so much bigger and better than mine. I see it this way:

If you can picture God looking down on us, watching and writing our stories as we go, He doesn't make choices for us because He loves us too much, but as He watches and waits, time is nothing but a background ticking noise from a giant wall clock. As it all stands still, in a split second, God sees every future outcome to the daily choices we make as we make them and the ripple effects those choices have on all those around us. And that's where He starts to rewrite multitudes of outcomes to all those effected from the ripple effects in the daily choices we humans make.

He writes our stories individually to always give us a way back to Him, ways to paths filled with grace and favor, paths that will cause us to prosper, paths that are filled with the Hope of the Lord God Almighty!

Every time I put him in a box, that's exactly the image I get of him rearranging the whole world in a split second because He cares that much about us individually it's not enough to just offer you a path to prosper in Him, but He rearranges so all those who are in the ripple effect also have the path to prosper in Him.

I've learned that we can't control any situation inflicted on us by someone else's bad choices, *but* we can choose to trust in our God to rewrite our futures and give us all the grace and favor needed to continue to stay on our own paths to destiny and finish the good works God started in us.

This is personal. It's not just for me. It's the same for you. God *will* finish the good work He started in you. Whatever the Enemy may be throwing at you in life today, just know that that's exactly what it is—it's thrown. It's nothing but a cheap shot because he knows it won't stick unless you let it. Because we may lose a battle from time to time in our fleshy lives, but ultimately God has won the war.

> O Lord, you hear the desire of the afflicted;
> you will strengthen their heart; you will incline
> your ear
> to do justice to the fatherless and the oppressed,
> so that man who is of the earth may strike terror
> no more.
> Psalm 10:17–18

Do you sometimes put God in a box because someone else's choices may have sideswiped you and left you crippled on your way to fulfilling the purposes God has for your life? Have you ever been left thinking, *That was it. It can't get any worse than this,* and then all of a sudden, an onslaught comes from the Enemy in all directions using the most unexpected people in your life to feed the fear inside you?

Well, my friend, I've been there, and my biggest weapon was recognizing these people aren't your enemy. My estranged husband wasn't my enemy. Call the Enemy out. Don't let the deception be a foothold for even a second.

Say it out loud and then go to the Word and speak out all those scriptures you have underlined, highlighted, stuck on your walls and the mirror, and speak the Word of God out loud over yourself, your circumstances, and the ones you love, even more so over the ones who are doing you wrong.

Then take a breath, stand still, and let God fight for you. He will and His word will cut through the Enemy's plans.

> But understand this, that in the last days there will come times of difficulty. For people will be lovers of self, lovers of money, proud, arrogant, abusive, disobedient to their parents, ungrateful, unholy, heartless, unappeasable, slanderous, without self-control, brutal, not loving good, treacherous, reckless, swollen with conceit, lovers of pleasure rather than lovers of God, having the appearance of godliness, but denying its power. Avoid such people. 2 Timothy 3:1–8

> The Lord tests the righteous,
> but his soul hates the wicked and the one who loves
> violence. Psalm 11:5

Do you not know that you are God's temple and that God's Spirit dwells in you? If anyone destroys God's temple, God will destroy him. For God's temple is holy, and you are that temple. 1 Corinthians 3:16–17

There are six things that the Lord hates, seven that are an abomination to him: haughty eyes, a lying tongue, and hands that shed innocent blood, a heart that devises wicked plans, feet that make haste to run to evil, a false witness who breathes out lies, and one who sows discord among brothers. Proverbs 6:16–19

Know this, my beloved brothers: let every person be quick to hear, slow to speak, slow to anger; for the anger of man does not produce the righteousness of God. James 1:19–20

All this to say, for some reason, all the fear I had was so overwhelming that I was choosing to keep the poison pumping into my veins rather than take the needle out. The poison of fear and shame was a constant drip, and my fear wasn't a fear of God but fear of man.

I didn't even realize until my eyes were opened by the Holy Spirit and God started to heal my heart, and the more I let Him into the damaged, dark, hurting places in my heart and soul, the more He soothed it with His word and His love.

God's works are miraculous, beautiful, and unfathomable. I cannot even try to put in words how He does what He does, but I know that I was clinging to the very thing God was tearing me away from because I was crippled with fear. It was when I released it to God and let it go that He took the time to gently work in me.

I look back as I type right now and I'm scrambling through

my phone to read the words that a stranger spoke over me as God whispered to my heart in April last year 2016.

Earlier on, I told a story of an encounter I had at a conference in March 2016 where God spoke to me about flourishing, and again months before that He had given me a vision of a single blooming flower in the dessert.

As I read the word spoken over me, I don't just see a single, stunning flower flourishing, but I see the potential of a whole field flourishing, blowing gently in sync of each other through a giant field surrounded by a white wooden picket fence. Inside that white wooden picket fence is where God is tending to His flowers, gently caring for them, and the flowers know no better, but each flower has been perfectly planted. And although they may not know their significance in this giant field, God is still caring for them ever so gently to ensure every single flower is flourishing in its own right that He made them for.

You see, you and I are the flowers, even if you don't yet believe.

You are well and truly God's daughters or sons, and He'll care for you in the shelter of His field and tend to you and watch over you.

God will make you brave, God will give you strength, God will take away your shame, and as He does, you will rise up like a beautiful blossoming flower facing the sun. In the same way the flower faces the sun, you will face Jesus, and if you keep your eyes fixed on Him and His word and let Him to continue to work on and in your life daily, the things of earth will grow strangely dim.

Do not let the Enemy distract you. Do not give him a foothold to bitterness, hate, or a hard heart. Keep your heart soft and know that while you live this life out honoring God He'll hold you up and fight for you.

Just be still and let Him fight for you.

> That according to the riches of his glory he may
> grant you to be strengthened with power through
> his Spirit in your inner being, so that Christ may

dwell in your hearts through faith that you, being rooted and grounded in love, may have strength to comprehend with all the saints what is the breadth and length and height and depth, and to know the love of Christ that surpasses knowledge, that you may be filled with all the fullness of God. Ephesians 3:16–21

Now to He who is able to do far more abundantly than all that we ask or think, according to the power at work within us, to Him be glory in the church and in Christ Jesus throughout all generations, forever and ever. Amen.

I have my own theory that the reason God whispers is because He is right there behind me or beside me, and I want to tell you that it's the same for you too. God is there right next to you; He is not ever far away enough to need to shout what He wants to say to you.

You just need to be still and wait on Him. Easier said than done, I know. It may have taken me eight years to learn how to be patient and wait on Him, but once you start, it becomes easier to slow down and make space for the one who took more than just time for us— He gave His own son's life as a sacrifice.

If you feel like you're drowning in your current circumstances and you cannot see the way out or up, hear my encouragement directly for you: it may feel like you're drowning, but if you call out to Jesus and focus on how big God is, He is bigger than whatever it is you're coming up against.

God won't let you drown. The waters might be sweeping around you, but they won't consume you. The storms in life won't stop. The Word says we will face trials and tribulations not might. *But* God promises not to leave nor forsake us, He goes before and behind you. He makes a way when you don't see how it is even possible.

When You're Between a Rock and a Hard Place
But now, God's Message,

the God who made you in the first place, Jacob,
the One who got you started, Israel:
"Don't be afraid, I've redeemed you.
I've called your name. You're mine.
When you're in over your head, I'll be there
with you.
When you're in rough waters, you will not go down.
When you're between a rock and a hard place,
it won't be a dead end—
Because I am God, your personal God,
The Holy of Israel, your Savior.
I paid a huge price for you:
all of Egypt, with rich Cush and Seba thrown in!
That's how much you mean to me!
That's how much I love you!
I'd sell off the whole world to get you back,
trade the creation just for you.
Isaiah 43:1–4

I can testify to this over and over again in the last three years of my life. It would feel like I'd hit a brick wall or dead end and there was no possible way of circumstances changing, let alone God using me for anything in the future. I could have chosen to stay there in defeat and listen to the lies of the Enemy. Don't forget that is exactly what they are—big fat ugly lies.

But I chose to fight with the weapons God gave me, prayer and His word. I'd search God's word and find my hope in Him, and I have the urgency to tell you to search for yourself in His word, the everlasting hope that He will finish the very good work He started in you just like He is in me. The very thing that you're facing right now that is trying to break you, God can turn around and use to make you.

I believed God's promises over my life, and when I look back now on the last three years and see the people that He surrounded me with and the work He did in my life to bring me to the place I'm at right now as I type these words to you, it actually blows my mind at how kind He is.

God is not an angry, judgmental, harsh-spoken person. He is a loving, kind Father who knows what is best for us and wants to get you to the place He has purposed you for in everyday life.

There is no end goal you hit at a certain age to be at a certain place or have a certain title, but let me tell you there's something God is stretching, growing, and preparing you for so that in the days, weeks, months, and years to come. As you walk this journey out, you'll leave a trail blazing behind you. Not a trail of mess and confusion, but a trail that burns bright like a heart on fire burning for Jesus, and all who see you will know that He is God, and He is good in your life.

You won't even need to tell people because they'll see, and once people see, they cannot unsee. You will find yourself in the paths of people who are a step behind you, and they need the hope or encouragement of what you have just walked through.

Don't hide or feel disqualified to give people hope in Jesus. Whatever shame you may feel, just remember Jesus took that shame on the cross, and He's the one who qualifies you. No man and no woman on this earth can disqualify you from what God is calling and equipping you for.

God will open the doors for you that need to be opened to get you to where he wants you if you're willing. You don't need to be able because when we are weak, He is strong and well able to work in and through you.

Sometimes I felt the need to have it all together, to strive for perfection and be invincible. I knew right from the beginning of the stormy season I found myself in that I'd not be a statistic or textbook turnout from my circumstances. I knew God would have me defy the odds and raise up above the circumstances I found myself forced into. But I still would at times be overcome with my humanness and feel the emotional roller coaster of doubt, fear, loneliness, and weakness.

I'd often forget that when I'm weak He is strong, but then the Holy Spirit would gently give me a nudge and remind me God is strong in my weakness. And it's in those moments that God would stretch me into uncomfortable and unknown. And that's where the beauty of blossoming faith in action has to kick in.

I cover myself and the kids more than once daily with the confessions of God's promises over our lives and His word. When I first started doing it over two years ago, it was like every confession out loud was a step in faith toward Jesus as he patiently waited with his hand stretched out to me ready and waiting to take me by the hand and out of the unknown toward His safety. I don't know how to explain it any other way. I was so scared of the unknown, but the only thing I knew to do was to trust God. Running to God was the only thing my mind, spirit and soul could make sense to do.

I tell you this because I want to encourage you that even when everything feels wrong and you cannot make sense of the reality around you, the one thing you can trust is God, and if you run to him and put God first, I guarantee you will never come second. God will raise you up with His very own mighty hand.

When All Is Said and Done

If there was something I could leave with you like we were having a catch up over coffee, I'd tell you:

I'm just a girl who loves Jesus more than anything else on this earth. And I realized as I started in the more recent years to become the woman God made me to be that He is just a God who loves me so much that He gave the ultimate sacrifice of His own son to take away all my sin, shame, sickness, and any debt the Devil will try to put on me.

Never give up and don't settle for less that God's promises over you.

When you don't feel like it the most, press in harder to God's word.

When the last thing you want to do is talk to anyone, take that as the very chance to get away quietly to pray and wait on the Holy Spirit.

When all you want to do is prove to the entire world you did good and right before God, breathe in focus back onto Jesus and remind yourself you don't need to prove anything to anyone. God will raise you up in His good and perfect timing.

My friend, as easy as it is to say, I know it's not as easy to do. *But* it is possible, and I can testify from my own life and experience you can trust God. He is the one you can fully rely on even when nothing makes sense and it feels like the world you have built around you is failing and falling down.

I look back now, and I'm grateful the walls I had built around my life crumbled and fell down because although I felt so raw, vulnerable, and so uncomfortable, I'd have never thought anyone could come out the other side of circumstances like mine.

God rebuilt walls with a firm foundation that the enemy cannot penetrate through and even the things that used to knock me down and out one brick at a time no longer stick when they are thrown my way. Ephesians 6:10–12

A Fight to the Finish

And that about wraps it up. God is strong, and He wants you strong. So take everything the Master has set out for you, well-made weapons of the best materials. And put them to use so you will be able to stand up to everything the Devil throws your way. This is no afternoon athletic contest that we'll walk away from and forget about in a couple of hours. This is for keeps, a life-or-death fight to the finish against the Devil and all his angels.

If you can forgive, love will truly win. Love never fails.

Printed in the United States
By Bookmasters